TRAINING DEVELOPMENT
GUIDE

Ronald I. Ribler

Reston Publishing Company
Reston, Virginia
A Prentice-Hall Company

Library of Congress Cataloging in Publication Data
Ribler, Ronald I.
　Training development guide.

　　1. Employees, Training of—Handbooks, manuals,
etc.　3. Training manuals.　I. Title.
HF5549.5.T7R439　1983　　　658.3′12404　　　82-10223
ISBN 0-8359-7791-9

© 1983 by
Reston Publishing Company, Inc.
Reston, Virginia 22090

10　9　8　7　6　5　4　3　2　1

Printed in the United States of America

Contents

PART 2: TRAINING DEVELOPMENT TASKS

Introduction

This Guide has been prepared for teachers, technicians, technical writers, and others who have had limited experience with the systematic development of training materials. It provides a step-by-step approach based on proven techniques currently being used successfully by many training professionals. The Guide is designed as an aid, rather than as a set of rules and standards. In short, it is intended to be a simplified, basic handbook.

The word *job* as it is used here, means any work, skill, or knowledge for which specific training or educational requirements have been identified.

There is extensive space for you to make notes as you read and use the Guide. The Guide, with your personal notes, can become a valuable reference whenever you find yourself tasked to develop training in the future.

PRELIMINARIES | Part 1

1

How People Learn

Let's take a brief look at the theoretical foundations and history of the training techniques and methods currently in use.

Although theories of learning abound, while each theory has considerable supporting research, none has been proven to be "correct" beyond question. Much of the theory in vogue today has its origins in Pavlov's conditioning experiments. The historic dog-bell-food model ascribed to Pavlov has evolved through the twentieth century into a highly complex and sophisticated set of theoretical constructs, generally known as Behaviorism. Today's best known Behaviorist is B. F. Skinner, who has been perhaps the most significant inspiration in the theory and practical application of learning principles.

The central construct of the Behaviorist is *reinforcement,* which is a reward for performance. For example, if you're teaching your pet dog to sit, you encourage, admonish, push, and do whatever you can until the animal understands your command. When the dog finally sits at your command, you shower approval, affection, and perhaps even food on him. Thus, he knows that his response of sitting to the stimulus of your vocal command was what you wanted. You have

3

reinforced his behavior by rewarding him with something pleasing. In simple terms, that is known as *positive reinforcement.*

The dog might have learned the sitting behavior even faster if you had struck him each time he didn't sit on your command. The reward, or reinforcement, in this case is the cessation of discomfort, which is known as *negative reinforcement.*

Negative reinforcement often leads to faster and perhaps more lasting learning, but is considered socially, morally, or even legally unacceptable in many cases. Negative reinforcement, while highly effective, is not condoned in free societies, with certain notable exceptions. Committing a felony in our society carries the threat of incarceration for long periods of time. Thus, the threat of prison is a negative reinforcement for lawful behavior and the threat of prison is a convincing deterrent to an overwhelming proportion of the citizenry. However, the prisons are bulging at the seams. Does that mean negative reinforcement doesn't work?

INDIVIDUAL DIFFERENCES

We've pointed out that reinforcement, positive or negative, doesn't explain all behavior. The prisons are full for many reasons—one is that some of the inmates prefer prison to the more threatening and uncomfortable life "outside." This concept—that people are different—is almost trite. Although it seems obvious, what is satisfying or rewarding to one person may be abhorrent to another. All people are not satisfied in the same ways nor are they rewarded by the same tokens.

MOTIVATION

The concept of individual differences leads directly into the concept of *motivation,* without which there would be no adult human learning. Motivation, although a commonly used term, has been the subject of countless research studies and essays, yet it remains largely a mystery. Motivation theories, like learning theories, are plentiful. We needn't be concerned with why people seem to have different motivations under similar circumstances. But we must understand and accept the proposition that people are different, and we cannot expect all people to have the same motivations.

Before going any further into this murky area, let's define the term motivation. *Motivation is an internal force that leads to establishment of satisfaction of some felt need by the individual.*

Motivation is *internal* to the individual. It isn't something one person gives to another. We all do whatever we do because we have a reason, even if that reason is unknown to us. If we are hungry, we seek food. Hunger is the motive; relief of the hunger becomes the object of our behavior. Therefore we can say that hunger causes us to seek food. The food itself is not a motivator; satisfaction of the hunger pangs is the motivation. Food is an *incentive* only. If we are hungry and are offered food for performing a pattern of behavior, we *may* perform that behavior to get the food, depending on the strength of the motivation and the strength of the incentive in our unique frame of reference. For example, if you offer a meal to a person who hasn't eaten for six hours if he would cut off his own finger, you wouldn't be surprised to have your offer rejected. However, if you offer that same person the same meal on the same terms after fifty hours without food, it might be accepted.

In training situations, we're usually not concerned with such severe situations, but we must always remember that what is attractive or necessary to one person may be rejected by another. You've probably heard, "I can't seem to motivate these people to work better." The person making that statement hasn't been able to figure out what rewards, or incentives, those people will respond to positively. The speaker feels that all the people in question will respond to the same incentives. The fact that the speaker has failed suggests that they will not all respond to the same incentives. Only some sales people, for example, will increase their sales activities if the incentive of increased commissions is offered. Others might perform at a higher level under contest conditions, while still others will not respond to any incentives because of an intense dislike of the sales manager.

The complexity of human beings and their interactions with their environment make it almost impossible to determine which incentives will be effective with which people, under which conditions, and at which times. How, then, can we approach training development for people we may not even know?

TRAINING PHILOSOPHY

We must assume that the people to be trained are willing to learn the skills and knowledge presented in the program. Even if this assumption is occasionally incorrect, if we were not to make it, to proceed with any training would be fruitless. *We must assume that the people to be trained are susceptible to the training.*

Some trainees will be more susceptible to training because of the importance of the material to *them*. Surgeons who are being trained in a technique to be used frequently will be more motivated to learn this skill than if they were being trained in the hospital's accounting practices. However, it may be necessary to train the surgeons in the hospital's accounting practices, and we must be able to capture their interest sufficiently to attain minimal goals.

Given at least minimum motivation to learn, we can enhance the level of motivation by tailoring the training to the individual student. Of course, we can't prepare separate training for each student, but we can strive to make the training fit the student *as the training progresses.* The techniques for approaching that goal are described in some detail in this Guide.

Permitting the trainee, within limits, to define the training needs and then work toward satisfying those needs is a cornerstone of the training philosophy woven through this text. Helping the trainees become aware of their own motivation aids them in focusing on the tasks at hand and in optimizing the energy required to learn the material.

The advent of self-paced, self-administered, and computer-aided instruction has given impetus to the development of related kinds of training.

When we tell learners what they're going to be learning, and then design instructional materials that address those objectives, the trainees become more willing to undertake the learning activities because they know what to expect. Fear of failure is reduced if the trainees are reassured that the objective is for them to succeed. The training philosophy in this Guide is that if the trainees fail to learn, the training is at fault, not the learners.

Getting Started

A point at which to begin the odyssey of training development is necessary. The journey from start to finish is often long and arduous, but you can increase your chances of success and minimize the time required to complete the effort if you find the starting point and proceed systematically through the development steps. There is no guarantee that you'll produce a usable training program by following the process in this Guide, but it is one way of getting the job done, and this method has been proven repeatedly.

While it may not be the most exciting job in the world, we have chosen to use the Mail Room Clerk as one of the examples used in the Guide. This job presents a set of functions and skills with which almost everyone is familiar.

Try to think of the relatively simple job of the Mail Room Clerk as a challenging and interesting training development assignment. If you've never developed a formal training program before, the challenge can be very real.

First, let's take a look at the job in some detail.

This job consists of selected mail room activities required to process both incoming and outgoing mail. The job involves use of a Zip Code Directory, a list of personnel, a Postal Services Manual, a postal scale, and a postage meter. The Mail Room Clerk must be able to operate the postal scale and the postage meter. The job excludes collecting mail from offices, but includes processing special delivery, registered, and certified mail; airmail; and parcels.

The next few pages develop the job description of the Mail Room Clerk. Read the job description carefully, and plan to reread it as you develop the training program. The job description is the basic resource document you'll use when developing training.

One final word before you begin—your own judgment is needed in generous doses whenever you're dealing with the intangibles encountered in a training program. Use your common sense to supplement the guidance offered here. These suggestions may not always fit specific situations; however, the logic and the systematic approach are the key ingredients to lead you through unfamiliar territory.

TASK 1. Process Incoming Mail

1. Sort out special mail. If addressee's name is not on personnel list, treat as undeliverable mail, and go to Task 1, Step 3b.

   1. Includes certified, registered, special delivery mail; and parcels.

2. Deliver special mail to individual addressee within one hour after sorting.

3. Sort regular mail.
   a. Put in bags according to floor.
   b. Put undeliverable mail in separate sack. If addressee's name is not on the list of personnel, call Personnel Department. Forward mail if address is available. Return mail to Post Office if addressee cannot be located.

   3. See Personnel List.

   3b. Task 2, Step 7.

4. Deliver bags to designated station on the appropriate floor.

TASK 1-1: Process Incoming Mail

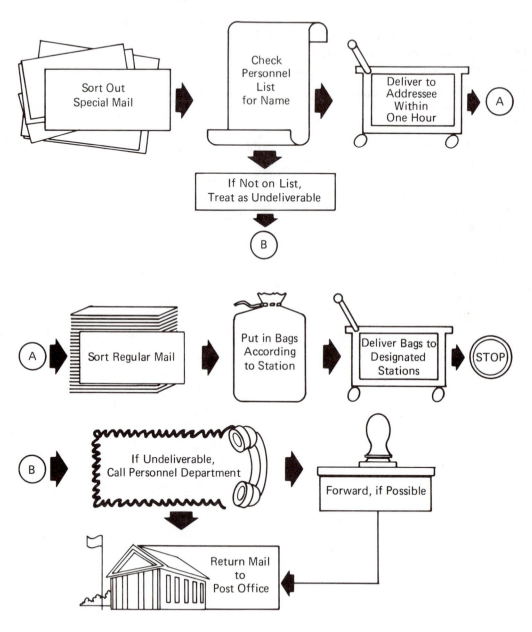

TASK 1-2: Sort Regular Mail

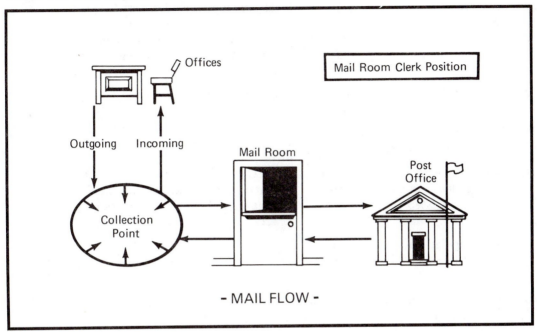

Offices

Mail Room Clerk Position

Outgoing   Incoming

Mail Room

Post
Office

Collection
Point

- MAIL FLOW -

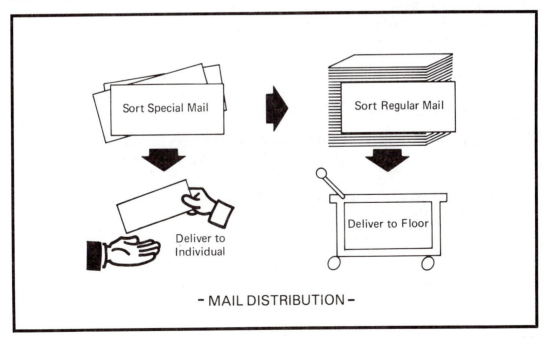

Sort Special Mail

Sort Regular Mail

Deliver to
Individual

Deliver to Floor

- MAIL DISTRIBUTION -

TASK 2: Process Outgoing Mail

1. Sort mail:
   a. Special mail.
   b. Airmail.
   c. Regular mail.

1. Special mail includes: certified, registered, special delivery, parcels. (Note: Unless marked air mail or as above, all mail will be regular first class.)

2. Check Zip Code on mail. If incomplete or missing, correct or add.

2. See Zip Code Directory.

3. Weigh regular and air mail using approved postal scale.

4. Check postage meter. If more postage is needed or if meter is broken, go to Task 3, Step 1.

4. CAUTION: The meter must have water, paper, and ink and must be plugged in before it will work properly.

5. Stamp regular and air mail using current rates listed in U.S. Postal Services Manual.

6. Bundle regular and air mail: local, out of town, air mail.

7. Deliver to Post Office:
   a. Post regular and air mail.
   b. Post special mail and get receipts.

8. Give special mail to supervisor.

TASK 3: Fill Postage Meter

1. If meter is broken or does not work properly, call Repair and report to supervisor who will supply stamps to use until meter is repaired. Go to Task 2, Step 5.

2. If meter is low, report to supervisor who will give you a check to cover the cost of refilling the meter.

3. Take postage meter to the Post Office to have it filled.

4. Give receipt for postage to your supervisor.

5. Go to Task 2, Step 5.

Before you begin the procedures outlined in this Guide, complete these four preparatory steps:

1. Define the job completely. This is the process involved in developing the job description. Each separate task is identified, and the steps necessary for its completion are listed in order. Refer to the example as you construct job descriptions.

2. Acquire a thorough understanding of the job. If possible, use firsthand observation and take careful notes. You may also use previously written job descriptions, existing manuals, and whatever other documents are available. Obviously, unless you're completely familiar with the tasks and the proper sequence of their performance, you won't be able to teach a trainee the most productive and efficient procedures to use on the job. Often, a training developer will have access to subject-matter experts, but we will assume, for the purposes of this book, that the person developing the training is also the subject-matter expert.

3. Define the population to be trained. What is the educational background of the trainees? How old are they? Do they have special language requirements or limitations? Are they moving up into jobs they already know a lot about? Or are they completely unfamiliar with the operation of the unit? Take these things into account as you construct the training package.

4. Identify required instructor qualifications. Will the instructor need to serve only as a guide through the training process, or is there need for a high level of technical background and experience? Will such experts be available to teach the course? Does the instructor need supporting materials, such as audiovisual aids, lesson plans, handouts, and questionnaires? Is it important for the instructor to have prior teaching experience? Experience on the job? All of these factors will affect the outcome of the training process.

The step-by-step development of training packages is shown in the accompanying illustration. The development procedure is identified by the sequence numbers, which should serve as guidelines for your first packages. After you've had some experience with the process, you may perform Tasks 2 through 5 in a different sequence than the one indicated, but it is *essential* that the remaining tasks be performed in the order shown. Task 7, particularly, should never be undertaken until the first six tasks are completed. There is a natural tendency to begin writing the training materials immediately but, more often than not, the result will be a waste of time and—perhaps worse—develop ineffective or irrelevant training. It's necessary to develop self-discipline and avoid the temptation to start at the wrong place. This is probably the most difficult aspect of the training development process, but if your objective is to produce sound, useful training materials, you should follow the sequence as illustrated.

USING THE GUIDE

Read the Guide through at least the first ten chapters of Part 2 before you begin developing training materials. The Guide will lead you though each phase of development. Refer to the Guide frequently and make notes.

When you're working on a training package, you may encounter questions that are not answered by this Guide. When you have a problem or simply have a question about the training package, a co-worker or supervisor often can provide the answers.

A number of forms are provided in this Guide. Make copies of the blank forms to use in your training materials development.

DEVELOPMENT OF TRAINING

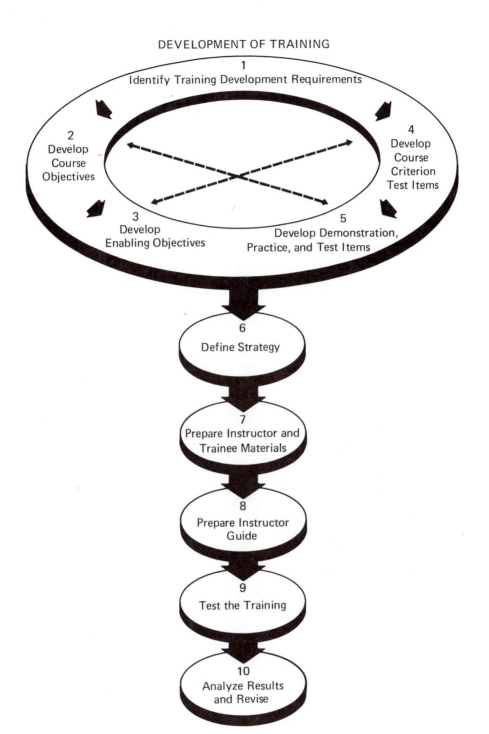

1
Identify Training Development Requirements

2
Develop
Course
Objectives

4
Develop
Course
Criterion
Test Items

3
Develop
Enabling Objectives

5
Develop Demonstration,
Practice, and Test Items

6
Define Strategy

7
Prepare Instructor and
Trainee Materials

8
Prepare Instructor
Guide

9
Test the Training

10
Analyze Results
and Revise

TRAINING DEVELOPMENT TASKS | Part 2

3

Task 1: Identify Training Development Requirements

In all job training, the primary objective is to train people to *perform* the job.

The first task of a training developer is to analyze the job to establish which skills and knowledge are necessary for its performance. This can be done by observation of a skilled incumbent or by diagramming the job. Refer again to the sample job description. From that diagram, you can identify what needs to be included in the training and what relevant skills and knowledge the trainee may have acquired previously.

Make a copy of the Training Requirements Form on the next page. The skills and knowledge requirements of the job should be listed under Column 1. A completed example of the same form for the job of Mail Room Clerk follows the blank form. Note the level of detail.

Several sources of information about the skills and knowledge that the students will bring to the training include: (a) a list of prerequisite courses and descriptions of the student population's skills and knowledge, and (b) the Task Analysis prepared earlier.

These items should be analyzed in terms of the entries made in Column 1 of the Training Requirements Form, with particular at-

DETERMINE SKILLS AND KNOWLEDGE TRAINEES WILL NEED

DETERMINE SKILLS AND KNOWLEDGE TRAINEES HAVE

TRAINING REQUIREMENTS FOR THE JOB OF _____

1	2	3	4
SKILLS AND KNOWLEDGE NEEDED TO PERFORM THE JOB (Describe)	SKILLS AND KNOWLEDGE THE TRAINEES HAVE (YES/NO)	ALTERNATIVES TO TRAINING (Define)	TRAINING REQUIREMENTS (1 − 2 + 3) (X)

TRAINING REQUIREMENTS FOR THE JOB OF ___Mail Room Clerk___

1	2	3	4
SKILLS AND KNOWLEDGE NEEDED TO PERFORM THE JOB (Describe)	SKILLS AND KNOWLEDGE THE TRAINEES HAVE (YES/NO)	ALTERNATIVES TO TRAINING (Define)	TRAINING REQUIREMENTS (1 – 2 + 3) (X)
Identify special delivery, certified, registered, air, and regular mail.	no		X
Use Zip Code Directory to obtain Zip Codes.	no		X
Use postal scale.	no	Job Aid	
Use and read postage meter.	no		X
Fill postage meter.	no		X
Determine postal rates for first class and air mail.	no	Job Aid	
Discriminate local, out of town, and air mail.	no		X
Where post office is located.	yes		

tention to how they relate to the work required in the job. Usually, it's possible to match existing skills and knowledge to those required, and to make entries in Column 2 that correspond to the requirements listed in Column 1. Only *relevant* skills and knowledge brought by the trainees should be considered.

As with the entries for Column 1, items may turn up later in the development process that should be entered in Column 2.

By looking at the Column 1 entries, you may determine that some of the requirements can be satisfied by the use of a training aid or other similar device. It may not be necessary to provide training for all the training requirements. For instance, presentation of a glossary during the training may be a sufficient substitute for teaching the terms that are essential to the performance of the job. Sometimes the alternatives to training will not become apparent until the materials development phase is reached, but when you encounter them, enter them in Column 3.

The entries on the Training Requirements Form will prove invaluable in later tasks to verify that all the requirements have been identified and addressed in the training package.

**DETERMINE
TRAINING
REQUIREMENTS**

After completing Columns 1–3, you'll see that some of the requirements in Column 1 are satisfied by entries in Column 2 and Column 3. The training requirements to be satisfied by the training package are those that remain. Thus, the entries in Column 4 represent only those identified requirements not accounted for by the entries in Columns 2 and 3.

**VERIFY
IDENTIFICATION
OF ALL TRAINING
REQUIREMENTS**

At this stage of the training development, most of the training requirements will have been determined, but others may not be discovered until later. At this point, however, verify that all of the known requirements are stated and that they are related to job performance. Time and money will be wasted unless the stated requirements are actually the ones for which the training is to be developed.

A supervisor or an associate familiar with the job should review your training requirements before you proceed. Have more than one person look at them to be sure you've captured the total requirements. This can save reworking the package later and make the entire task simpler.

4

Task 2: Develop Course Objectives

Statements of objectives for the development of a training course should express the *performance* expected of the trainees upon completion of the program. The end-of-course objectives are stated in terms of *observable behavior* or *performance,* and do not simply describe what the trainees have learned.

A thorough analysis of the job is required to determine what behavior is necessary to perform the job completely and correctly. The training requirements analysis is the input to the process of developing objectives.

The second essential element in the definition of objectives is that they allow for *measurement.*

Thus, the essential features of objectives statements are that they are *observable* and *measurable.*

All objectives should include:

1. An input, or condition.

2. Disposition of the input, or how the condition is to be handled.

3. Performance criteria.

4. Disposition of the output, or result of the actions taken.

All the necessary information should be contained in the job description, in the task analysis, and in the training requirements analysis results.

In virtually all jobs, there is an input or initial condition with which the trainee will have to do something. When you've identified the input or condition, it becomes the first part of the objective. For example:

"Given the day's incoming mail . . ."
"Given the day's outgoing mail . . ."
"Given a postage meter . . ."

These kinds of opening phrases express the input or condition part of the objective.

Task statements in the job description should define the action required for different inputs or conditions. Most, if not all, of the course objectives will be related to the task statements in the job description. They should be expressed in enough detail so that there can be no doubt of the meaning.

Here again, the job description is the source of the required information. This part of the objective statement identifies the specific action, decision, or process required of the trainee.

Examples of this segment of the statement are:

". . . will process according to the job description . . ."
". . . will process according to the job description . . ."
". . . will get it filled . . ."

Always state this part of the objective in terms of measurable performance. Use action verbs. In the long run, how well the objective is stated will determine whether or not the student has learned to perform.

Some job tasks will require that something be done with the output. However, most tasks and, therefore, most objective statements don't require information regarding what is done with the output. In this case, the completion of the process outlined previously will usually give the complete objective statement.

Putting together two of the examples already given, we have:

"Given the day's outgoing mail, the trainee will process it according to the job description."

This is a statement of the objective in behavioral terms—the expected behavior is observable and measurable. The trainee must make a decision before processing the input, and we can measure that performance by presenting the learner with such a request and then determining if the mail is processed correctly.

Some job tasks will call for disposition of the processed input. In such cases, the objective statement should include that action. To continue the examples:

"... and deliver it to the post office."
"... and deliver it to the designated station on the appropriate floor."

DETERMINE THE OUTPUT OR RESULT OF EACH PROCESS

Each objective should be examined to determine whether this part of the statement is actually required.

Again, it's important to remember that all parts of the objective should be expressed in *observable* and *measurable* terms.

The examples of course objectives below exemplify the differences between good and poor objectives.

EXAMPLES OF COURSE OBJECTIVES

Good	*Poor*
1. Given the day's outgoing mail, process it according to the job description and deliver it to the Post Office. *Criterion:* 100 pieces of mail per hour with an error rate not to exceed one percent.	1. Know how to process outgoing mail.
2. Given the day's incoming mail, process it and deliver it to the designated station on the appropriate floor. *Criterion:* 100 pieces of mail per hour with an error rate not to exceed one percent.	2. Understand how to process incoming mail.
3. Given a postage meter, get it filled when necessary. *Criterion:* Never run the meter so low that the day's mail will be delayed.	3. Learn how to get a postage meter filled.

Using the process just described, each objective should be written so it expresses the *behaviors* to be trained. Often there will be about the same number of objectives as tasks in the job, but this will depend on the job structure. When the list of course objectives is com-

WRITE COURSE OBJECTIVES IN MEASURABLE TERMS

plete, it should represent all of the new behaviors expected of the trainee at the end of the course.

When you've finished writing your of course objectives, you should check again to be certain your coverage is complete. This is a good time to go back and look at your training requirements analysis and your completed job description.

5

Task 3: Develop Enabling Objectives

Enabling objectives are related to, and often are derived from, the course objectives. They're usually expressed in a more detailed form and are addressed to the instructional unit, rather than to the entire course. They define for the trainee the information and knowledge needed to perform the tasks of the job. Enabling objectives are not usually tested at the end of the course, since they simply enable the trainee to perform the tasks necessary to be able to perform the tasks defined by the course objectives. An example of the derivation of enabling objectives from course objectives is shown below.

Course Objective

Given the day's outgoing mail, process it according to the job description.

Enabling Objectives

1. Upon completion of this unit, you will be able to sort, without error, twenty-five pieces of the day's outgoing mail in

27

fifteen minutes. You will sort the mail into groups of special delivery, certified, registered, air, and regular mail.

2. When you complete this unit, you'll be able to correct or add Zip Codes to the day's outgoing mail, using a Zip Code Directory.

3. Given mail of different weights, you'll be able to demonstrate how to weigh the pieces accurately on a postal scale.

4. Given the day's outgoing mail, you'll be able, in one hour and with ninety-nine percent accuracy, to sort one hundred pieces of mail into packets of local mail, out-of-town mail, and air mail.

As you can see, it would be impossible for the trainee to meet the criteria for the course objective without being able to satisfy the criteria defined in the enabling objectives. Therefore, if the trainee can perform the course criteria, you can assume the criteria for the enabling objectives have been satisfied.

Another way to define enabling objectives is to state that they ensure the requisite skills and knowledge needed to perform the more encompassing course objectives.

Task 4: Develop Course Criterion Test Items

Course criterion test items measure whether, or to what extent, the course presentation satisfied the course objectives. In other words, the course criterion test gauges how effective the course has been in doing it's intended job.

Course criterion test items are designed to measure trainee performance, and should be expressed in terms of performance rather than knowledge. For example, the criterion test item will ask the trainee to complete a process to determine if he or she can perform the task. The test doesn't ask the trainee for information about the process. The essence of the criterion test item is that it asks the trainee to *perform,* not just to show knowledge. Regardless of what subject is being trained, demonstration of the application by performance is a more accurate and meaningful measure of learning than the simple regurgitation of facts. Certainly none of us would have much confidence in a pilot who learned to fly from a book and had never been in the cockpit of an airplane.

Trainee performance is based on the tasks of the job that require the trainee to demonstrate some skill. These tasks or skills are reflected in the course objectives.

DETERMINE THE PERFORMANCE REQUIRED

It's usually sufficient to match the criterion test item directly to the objective. For example, a course objective might be stated as: "Upon completion of the course, the trainee will be able to correctly process incoming and outgoing mail." It will then be possible to establish criterion test items that measure whether or not, or how well, the trainee can process incoming and outgoing mail.

When we specify the accuracy levels required of any objective, we are identifying those that are required in the job. As in the course objectives, the test items should realistically match the requirements of the job. In the example given, the performance required is to "correctly process incoming and outgoing mail."

When you've determined the required performance for the first item, write it down. Then number it and enter, in the Criterion Test Item Log, the information you have up to this point. In this case, you have Criterion Test Item 1, so you'll enter a 1 in Column 1.

It's usually possible to match the test item to a specific task or set of tasks in the job description. If you can determine this now, enter the reference by task number in Column 2. You'll complete the remainder of the columns as you proceed with your program development.

When the Log is completed, it will provide a useful reference. It can help you ensure that all relevant elements of the testing are included in the package. You'll use this form throughout the course development process.

PREPARE COURSE CRITERION TEST ITEMS

Now that you've determined what the required performance is that you'll be testing, you're ready to prepare a test item. If, as in our earlier example, you're dealing with mail processing, you'll need to test the trainee on all aspects of the process. For example, before the trainee can process mail, he or she should be able to recognize the different types of mail. Your test item then might be: "Take one hundred pieces of outgoing mail from the bin and sort them, in one hour, into stacks of regular, air, special delivery, certified, and registered mail."

This kind of criterion test item should be prepared so that it measures the trainee's ability to process the mail through all possible paths defined by the job description. If there are many paths, test each one separately. Parts common to several paths may be tested only once. In the same way, there may be too many actions in the job to test them all. Then you must select representative items that test the trainee's ability to perform the tasks. Here are some examples of appropriate course criterion test items:

1. Here is a stack of mail. Treat it as incoming mail and process it as you would on the job. You may refer to your job description and any other available aids. Do not actually distribute the mail.

CRITERION TEST ITEM LOG

CRITERION TEST ITEM NUMBER 1	POSITION DOCUMENT REFERENCE 2	OBJECTIVE NUMBER 3	SCORING CRITERIA 4

2. Here is another stack of mail. Treat this stack as outgoing mail, processing it as you would on the job. You may refer to your job description or your available aids. Do not take the mail to the Post Office.

Now return to the paper on which you wrote the performance requirements and complete the test item. You can also make entries in the Criterion Test Item Log at this time. In this instance, you could make an entry in Column 4 if you have determined that a passing performance requires that all processes be completed correctly. Repeat the process until you've completed all the course criterion test items. Refer to the example of a Criterion Test Item Log for the Mail Room Clerk.

**REVISE COURSE
CRITERION TEST
ITEMS**

Make any revisions, additions, or deletions that result from your review of the course criterion test items now. This is a very important step because a great deal of the course development work to come depends heavily on good course criterion test items. Critical examination of the test items often brings up ideas you may not have considered before.

Be certain that all the items are completed and understandable. Associates or supervisors who may be completely unfamiliar with the job can help because their lack of familiarity with the job helps them to judge if your test items are stated clearly.

**COMPARE
COURSE
OBJECTIVES TO
CRITERION TEST**

Now make certain your course criterion test items support the course objectives. Each objective must relate to its criterion test item, and vice versa. Often there may be more than one test item to an objective. Entries in Columns 2 and 3 of the Criterion Test Item Log should be completed so you can see whether you have included all the objectives and criterion test items. This is a good opportunity to check the objectives and the test items against the job tasks, as defined in the job description. This check often leads to a better match between the objectives and the test items.

There may be too many or too few items, or they may address the wrong things. Take the time now to make the necessary adjustments and changes.

CRITERION TEST ITEM LOG

CRITERION TEST ITEM NUMBER 1	POSITION DOCUMENT REFERENCE 2	OBJECTIVE NUMBER 3	SCORING CRITERIA 4
1	TASK ANALYSIS TASK 2; Outgoing mail.	1	100 pieces/hour at 99% accuracy
2	TASK ANALYSIS TASK 1; INCOMING mail.	2	100 pieces/hour at 99% accuracy
3	TASK ANALYSIS TASK 2, step 4.	3	Meter never runs to zero.
4	TASK ANALYSIS TASK 1, step 3; Sort incoming mail.	4	25 pieces correctly in 15 minutes with no errors.
etc.			

7

Task 5: Develop Demonstration, Practice, and Test Items

The concept of job training includes the following elements:

1. A standard introduction of course material, presenting the instruction in the form of demonstration or explanation.

2. Trainee practice of the activity.

3. A test to determine if the trainees can perform the tasks that were taught.

You have already completed the course criterion test items and have defined the enabling objectives. The results of those two activities provide the basis for the information you require to complete the demonstration, practice, and test items. The definition of the unit structure in Task 6 will give you the specific points in the training where these items are to be applied. Here are some examples of the sequence of demonstration, practice, and test items:

DEMONSTRATION ITEM

A Zip Code contains *five* digits.
The numbers 90014, 22305, and 48640 are all Zip Codes.

This information could be presented as text, written on a chalkboard, or projected onto a screen.

PRACTICE ITEM
(the same basic information)

Circle the five-digit numbers:

12346	16102
2901	00031
92	1982

Circle the numbers below that could be Zip Codes:

18021	19
16102	933-34
2901B	18888

Responses to these instructions are usually given on paper, but may be delivered orally.

TEST ITEM
(the same basic information)

Which of the following could be Zip Codes?

43210	2836
1621	28
80190	1491
658876	1234G
12K34	12-980
77222	33333

Tests may be administered in many forms. It's advisable to retain records of test results.

A good general rule in constructing test items is to proceed from the simple to the more complex examples in the demonstration. Normally, it isn't so important for the practice items to begin at the same simple level as the demonstration items. The test items should be representative of all the elements of the skills and knowledge being measured. The most difficult of the unit test items should be as challenging as the comparable course criterion test items.

Careful study of these examples will help you understand how these items are constructed. It's often a good idea to develop the test item first. That way, you have a clear picture of where you expect the trainee to be, and you can prepare the demonstration and practice items based on the trainee's expected final performance. In this case, the demonstration item is based on the test item.

The practice items include variations. Practice items generally include more detail than test or demonstration items. All of these items are very important to the training, and the feedback to the trainees during the course presentation provides perhaps the most significant part of the learning experience. Feedback is discussed in more detail in Tasks 7 and 8.

When you've completed all the demonstration, practice, and test items, compare them with the course criterion test items and with the enabling objectives. You should recognize the tasks to be performed in each item, and should ask the trainee for performance of the same observable and measurable (skills and knowledge) behaviors.

PREPARE ENABLING TEST ITEMS

You developed the course criterion test items in Task 4. You've also developed enabling objectives. Now you'll use them to construct your enabling test items.

Write your enabling test items to match the course criterion test items and the enabling objectives. Write one test item for each of the enabling objectives. Next, review the entire test to determine if you need any more items to make the test complete. Certain activities may have variations that will require more than one item to test whether or not the trainees have achieved a given objective.

PREPARE ENABLING DEMONSTRATION AND PRACTICE ITEMS

Once you have developed all the necessary test items, you're ready to write the practice and demonstration items. As you've already seen, these items are similar to the test items and derive readily from them. There usually are more practice items than any other type, since these provide most of the skill development or knowledge drill. The trainees use the practice items to learn the detailed step-by-step procedures required to perform the job elements. Therefore, you'll need to break the test items into their basic components so the trainees can practice each part until they can, ultimately, perform all elements of the job, as represented by the test items. The last practice item should be similar to the test item. This aids the trainees in preparing for the test and helps build confidence, which often leads to better performance. Repeat the process until you have written all practice items relating to all test items.

Review your practice items for completeness and consistency. Revise them as necessary. Be sure to prepare a list of correct answers for all items. These answers will be included in the instructor's materials and in other forms for feedback to the trainees.

The next step is to derive the demonstration items from the practice items. This is done in the same way the practice items were derived from the test items. Many of the demonstration items will be oriented toward the enabling objectives.

The most important purpose of the demonstration items is to convey to the trainees the information needed to perform the tasks of the job. These will use the job aids and other available resources, some of which you'll develop as part of the training program. In writing the demonstration items, pay special attention to the understanding and knowledge the trainees will require to perform the practice and test items. Look at the practice items to find which of the enabling objectives must be reached in the demonstration items. Continual checking of the practice items against the demonstration items and the enabling objectives is necessary if the practice items are to be complete and consistent.

When you've finished these activities, make one more check of the entire set of test, practice, and demonstration items and hold them for sequencing in the next task.

The course materials will be built around the items you've just completed. If you've been thorough, the remaining work will be much simpler. This is a good time to review your work with an associate or with someone who has completed the training development process.

8

Task 6: Define Strategy

The strategy statement describes how you're going to approach the problem of presenting material to the trainees so that they will develop the required skills and knowledge. As you proceed through this task, you'll find the Strategy Checklist useful for guidance and for tracking what you're doing.

In this task you'll determine how the required information will be presented: in a self-instructional format, lecture, seminar, etc. This decision may have already been made for you, but there may be situations in which you should recommend an alternative.

ESTABLISH INSTRUCTIONAL MODE

Some criteria for the recommendation and selection of instructor-led versus self-administered instructional modes are as follows.

If the program is to be instructor-led:

1. Instructor expertise is required.

2. Interaction with students is necessary.

3. A lock-step method is desired, i.e., all students proceed together.

4. The program will be taught few times.

If the program is to be self-administered:

1. The student population should be large or geographically scattered.

2. The population probably will be heterogeneous.

3. The subject matter may be too personal for classroom application.

4. Pre-course orientations are required.

5. Time and facilities constraints do not permit an instructor-led format.

6. Replacement training of a substantial number of people in many locations is needed.

7. Availability of instructors is limited over an extended period of time.

The above criteria are offered for general guidance and should not be treated as a set of rules. Many other factors may influence your selection of the instructional mode, such as complexity or difficulty of the material, or costs. For example, the cost for developing good self-instructional materials can be much higher than the development of instructor-led materials, but self-instructional materials often represent a later saving in money, and instructor and student time. At times there are advantages to preparing the program using the instructor-led format and, after testing and shakedown, converting it for self-administered application. Your final decision may require consultation with associates who have made this kind of decision previously.

**DETERMINE
CLASS SIZE**

In your earlier data collection, you established how many people require training. You used that information to establish the instructional mode, and you'll use it now to help you to structure and schedule the course and the resources required.

Since procedures for training will vary in the field, when you establish the typical class size, you'll also be establishing the ideal trainee-instructor ratio. That ratio is dependent on: (a) the mode of instruction, (b) the nature of the content, and (c) the presentation media.

**IDENTIFY LEVELS
OF TRAINING
REQUIRED**

Several types of teaching are involved in skills training. In developing your strategy, it's useful to categorize job tasks into different behaviors and then to classify them into groups. The following sections define the major behavior groupings and should progress from the simple to the complex.

STRATEGY CHECKLIST

ITEMS	NOTES
1. Mode of presentation (check those that apply) ___ Instructor-led ___ Self-administered ___ Seminar ___ Other (specify). 2. Trainee/Instructor Ratio Number of instructors = ___ Number of trainees = ___ Ratio = ___ 3. Training Strategy ___Discrimination ___Concepts ___Chaining ___Principles ___Problem Solving. 4. Media ___Overheads ___Flipcharts ___35mm. slides ___Slide-tape ___Videotape ___Film ___Computer aided ___Other (specify). 5. Sequence Describe, in terms of objectives. 6. Elements Requiring Emphasis (list, in terms of objectives.) 7. Target Population ___Reading level ___Educational level ___Motivational level ___Other factors (specify). 8. Method of Presentation ___Simulation ___Using real equipment and situations ___Other (specify).	

Discriminations

Discrimination tasks are those that require a response or several different responses. For example, one task of the Mail Room Clerk is to discriminate between local, air, and out-of-town mail. The input is the outgoing mail; the response is sorting according to the defined categories. The training strategy for this type of behavior should be to show, prompt, and solicit the response; and then to repeat. After one or two cycles the prompting is withheld and the trainee practices the task. Finally, the test is given, and the training for the task is complete. The same strategy should be followed for more complicated discriminations, though these may require more demonstration, practice, and exercise for the trainee to master.

Concepts

Concepts, as well as discriminations, must be learned for the successful performance of many tasks. The strategy for teaching the concept of the Zip Code involves more than just its format. It includes the introduction of the concept by describing it in terms the trainees can understand and put into practice. You should also give the trainees examples that may or may not fit the definition of the concept, and then ask for the correct response. Sometimes, the trainees do not necessarily have to know *why* certain things are done to perform the job tasks. Thus, *if certain concepts are not necessary to job performance, they should not be taught.*

Chaining

Many jobs require trainees to perform the tasks in a fixed sequence or set of sequences, using behavior previously learned and supplemented by the contents of the position. For example, the Mail Room Clerk position uses the trainee's ability to read addresses on mail, and adds sequencing and other elements to that basic ability. Training of this type is called chaining, which employs the following progressive strategy:

1. Present the trainee with an overview, or "walk through," of the chain, with no recall expected.
2. Follow by instruction in units of the chain which are not present in the initial repertoire of the trainee.
3. Teach the trainee to perform the elements of the chain in the required order; have the trainee practice to ensure that the sequence is fixed in his or her performance.

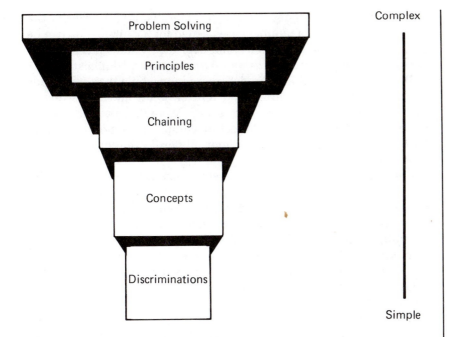

Complex

Problem Solving

Principles

Chaining

Concepts

Discriminations

Simple

TRAINING STRATEGIES

Principles

Another level of training deals with principles, which are chains of concepts. When there is a need for principles, there is a prerequisite need for concepts. The strategy for teaching principles is to explain to the trainee, in specific terms, what result is expected from the instruction. Then demonstrate the principle by example. The trainee should be supported in the practice activities via prompting.

Problem Solving

Problem solving is the application of previously learned principles and concepts in a new way to solve a specified type of problem. The strategy for teaching problem solving is to present simple problems and to progress to more difficult ones requiring the application of concepts and principles at an increasingly complex level. This continues until the trainee can perform the problem solving aspects of the job.

The term *media* refers here to audiovisual aids employed with some form of text to accomplish the objectives of the training program. Visual materials shown via an overhead projector are commonly

DETERMINE MEDIA

used in job training. They require considerable attention from the instructor and, if large numbers are needed for a course, they can be awkward to use. On the other hand, overhead visuals have the advantage of being relatively inexpensive and easy to duplicate.

Photographic slides are simpler to use in teaching than overheads because slides don't require so much attention from the instructor. On the other hand, they are more expensive to make and are not as easily duplicated or revised. Projection equipment is more expensive for 35mm slides, especially when multiple projection or random access is required.

Self-contained audiovisual presentations (slide-tape, filmstrip-tape, etc.) are much more expensive and difficult to produce and change than either the overheads or the 35mm slides. Self-contained audiovisual presentations are usually prepared when the material is not subject to substantial change and when other types of training media have already been used to validate the training.

You may choose from a wide range of media. Consult with audiovisual experts before making final decisions to use extensive audiovisual materials.

The correct media selection at this point prevents problems later. When you know the media you're going to use, you'll be careful to ensure that they don't interfere with or overpower the presentation of the subject matter. For example, too many overhead visuals in a short period of time can consume the instructor's time and energy. Conversely, the trainees may become bored while a single image remains on the screen, thus detracting from the presentation. Conditions will vary from one course to another, but a good general rule is to allow each image to be displayed only so long as it's useful. You'll want to avoid losing the trainees' interest or diverting their attention.

The ultimate criterion for media selection should be that the media provide the best training within existing constraints. The term media is a plural, suggesting that you'll probably want to use more than one medium in your training materials. For many instructor-led courses, the simpler media may be used during trial presentations. As the training program matures and the requirements are validated, other media may become more appropriate.

**ESTABLISH
SEQUENCE**

Instructional sequence is an important element of training development because it has an impact on the response of the trainees to the presentation. Your material should flow in a rational and systematic manner, with the logic apparent to the trainees.

Sequencing course material often requires little more than following the sequence of the job tasks. Some jobs, however, involve so many branches that the sequence may be difficult to detect or to follow. In such cases, look for elements of the position that are generic, or common to several tasks, and, if they are preliminary activities of the job, teach them early in the course.

For positions which include several types of inputs, conditions, or processing, the best approach generally is to sequence the steps for each type. For example, if the job involves the receipt of an input under a given set of conditions, and if a condition varies, the processing may also vary. Thus there may be more than one way to process a given input to this job.

You should establish the sequence so that each type of input, condition, and process is handled separately. The trainees may become confused if more than one way to do the work is shown at the same time. This process may help create generic modules for early steps in the instructional sequence that reduce repetition and enhance the instruction of the remaining, necessary parts of the material.

You should also remember another, oft-repeated guideline for sequencing the course material: *proceed from the simple to the complex, and from general to specific material.*

You now have several guidelines for sequencing the material to be taught:

1. Isolate common elements.

2. Follow inputs through the job one at a time.

3. Proceed from the general to the specific.

4. Proceed from the simple to the complex.

Note your selected sequence on the Strategy Checklist and use it in the definition of lesson unit structure. Lesson units frequently follow the job description, but there will be exceptions, just as for the basic sequencing. A major determinant of unit structure is length. You should be able to complete a unit of instruction in one session. Actual unit time may vary from a few minutes to a half day, but usually should not extend beyond that.

If you include too many tasks or major concepts in a unit, trainees may be confused, and little or no learning will be accomplished. The key is to make the contents of the unit significant—to the job and to the learner. Use the same kind of reasoning you applied to the development of the job description, where each task usually represents one major activity or concept. Design the unit to follow the task structure, within any constraints established by your sequencing. Several instructional units may be required where many alternatives are possible, or complex processing of input materials or data is required.

Some tasks may be simple enough that several may be combined into a single instructional unit. Unit structure is largely a matter of your judgment and knowledge of the job, but generally the structure is determined by some combination of:

1. The number and complexity of the tasks in the job.

2. The length of time required for presentation.

3. A rational breaking point.

After you've defined the course structure and created instructional units, your next step is to match the course objectives to the unit structure. You must establish which objectives are to be satisfied in each unit of instruction. Using completed job descriptions and Strategy Checklists along with your list of course objectives, and your Table of Objectives, list the course objective numbers on the Table of Objectives. Using the Strategy Checklist, Section 5, with the items mentioned above, note the corresponding unit number alongside each course objective. Be sure that all objectives are included on the list and matched to the units before proceeding.

Now, look at the Training Requirements Form and define the objectives in precise terms. For example, in the sample Training Requirements for Mail Room Clerk, the trainees must use a Zip Code Directory to obtain correct Zip Codes. This must be expressed in terms of an enabling objective, or a series of them.

Match each enabling objective to the units in which they will be taught. Enter the unit numbers on the Objectives Form. Be certain you have included all the enabling objectives, assigned to units.

Be sure that the enabling objectives are complete and consistent and that you've entered them all on the Objectives Form. The relationships between the course and the enabling objectives should be clear, and you should be able to see which match each unit. If the entries on the Objectives Form are not in unit sequence, arrange them so they may be readily used in the next steps of course development.

**IDENTIFY
ELEMENTS
REQUIRING
EMPHASIS**

Material requiring emphasis in the course presentation may be:

1. Important to the job.

2. So difficult that it requires drill and practice.

3. Similar to other activities to be performed in a job so the trainees must learn to differentiate among them to perform the task.

4. Illogical, in the remainder of the job.

In determining which points require emphasis, apply your knowledge of the job and consider the importance of the various job activi-

OBJECTIVES

COURSE OBJECTIVE NUMBER	UNIT NUMBER	ENABLING OBJECTIVE NUMBER	UNIT NUMBER

ties. You need to be concerned with the impact of actions required in the job as related to other associated jobs.

At this point in the development process, it's important to list the points requiring emphasis so you'll have them available for use later. List them in Section 6 of the Strategy Checklist. It's possible that some jobs will contain elements requiring little or no special emphasis, while others may include only one or two points.

Carefully examine elements of the job in which trainee performance can have a serious impact on other jobs. At this stage of development, it's better to err by including too many items for emphasis than to omit any. You'll resolve the matter when you begin to create the course materials themselves. The inclusion of too much prescribed practice will become apparent during the initial training tryouts.

ESTABLISH METHODS OF PRESENTATION

Although it is ideal to do so, you may not be able to train in the real environment where the job will be performed. You may, therefore, need to be inventive and establish presentation methods that approximate or simulate the real job environment.

Your decision to use a simulation method for training will depend on conditions that you expect to exist at the time of the initial presentation. Determine what those conditions will be, and make your decision based on this information. Several simulation methods are described in Tasks 5 and 7. Make an appropriate entry in Section 8 of the Strategy Checklist.

You'll have the course strategy and structure completed when you've filled in all the blanks on the Strategy Checklist. You'll be using the Checklist in later tasks in your course development. It's a good idea to review all your work to this point. If you have an opportunity, review the Strategy Checklist and the remainder of your materials with a colleague who has completed an activity similar to yours. It's often helpful to present your preliminary design to someone completely unfamiliar with the job or with training development. The naive reviewer can often point out potential sources of difficulty. In any event, this is the time for a careful review, even if you must do it yourself.

9

Task 7: Prepare Instructor's and Trainee's Materials

All the work you've done so far will serve as the input to the instructor's and trainee's materials. You'll prepare the course materials to ensure that the trainees develop the ability to meet the course objectives, as demonstrated by their mastery of the job activities. Trainees' successful performances on the tests indicate that the objectives have been met. Course development now proceeds to the preparation of the introduction and the first unit of instruction, as defined in Task 6. You'll prepare the course administration material in Task 8.

Locate the test, demonstration, and practice items, arranged by unit, that you prepared in Tasks 5 and 6. They'll be your guide to the preparation of the instructor's and the trainee's materials.

Select the test, demonstration, and practice items you plan to use in Unit 1, and review them to be certain you know exactly what the unit is to accomplish. Study the output of the enabling objectives (from Task 3) to be sure they're clear in your own mind. Recheck your strategy from Task 6 and make any adjustments you feel are necessary. If all your thoughts and materials are in order, you're now ready to begin writing the instructor's and trainee's materials.

The course introduction tells the students what to expect and gives the instructor last minute instructions for the course presentation. The introduction should include:

1. The relationship of the job to the organization of all related jobs or to the system in which it may be embedded.

2. The work of the job.

3. The course objectives.

4. An outline of the course activities.

Look at the sample course introduction. It's a typical example of the kind of introduction used in an instructor-led course.

COURSE INTRODUCTION EXAMPLE

Say: We're now ready to begin the course on how to process incoming and outgoing mail.

Do: Turn on projector and display visual A-2.

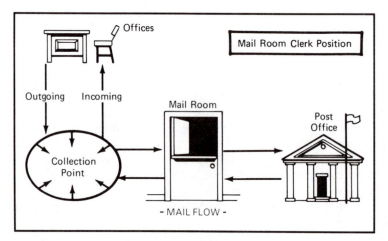

VISUAL A-2

Say: Here you can see how the Mail Room Clerk job fits into the overall organization of mail flow.

Do: Point to each position on the visual as you speak.

Say: Mail collection people pick up the *outgoing* mail in the offices twice each day and bring it to the mail room. Your job begins at this point, and ends when you deliver the mail to the Post Office.

As you can see, *incoming* mail originates at the Post Office, is processed by you, the Mail Room Clerk, and is eventually delivered to the individual offices.

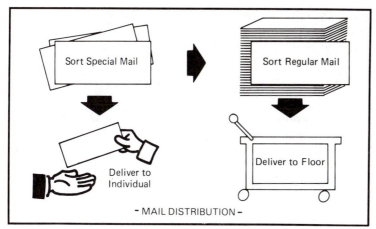

VISUAL A-3

Do: Project visual A-3.

Say: This diagram illustrates the major steps in Task 1—sorting *incoming* mail.

Do: Point to the steps on the visual as you describe them.

Say: You'll sort the mail according to type. Special mail is sorted out and delivered to the addressees. Then regular mail is sorted, put into bags according to floor, and delivered to designated stations. Later, we'll go into greater detail on the steps of each task.

You've just seen a typical opening segment, containing the kinds of material and information that should be included in your introduction.

It's most important that the language you use is comfortable for the trainees. Avoid unnecessary technical terms, and avoid jargon whenever you can, especially in the introductory segments of the training. In many cases, the trainees won't understand the meaning of terms such as objectives, criteria, unit, or module. These terms should almost always be introduced and explained if they're to be used, or other words should be substituted. You'll see some examples in the next section.

The instructor's materials for each unit should always begin with a statement of the objectives in terms that are meaningful to the trainees. If you examine the list of enabling objectives, you'll probably realize that they need rephrasing to make them meaningful to the trainees. For example, if the enabling objective states, "Given mail with incomplete or missing Zip Codes, the trainees will correct or add the Zip Codes." A better statement of the unit objective, from

**WRITE UNIT 1:
INSTRUCTOR'S
MATERIALS**

the trainee's point of view would be, "Now we're going to learn how to correct or add Zip Codes."

Following are some examples of trainee-oriented objectives statements.

Note: State each objective immediately prior to the instruction relating to it. Don't give the trainees a list of objectives; it will have little or no meaning to them at this point unless they have learned about objectives and their value already.

Objectives Statements Suitable for Trainees

1. We're going to learn how to:
   A. Bundle mail according to postal regulations.
   B. Fill a postage meter.
   C. Recognize an incomplete Zip Code.
   D. Use the Zip Code Directory.

2. When we complete this part of the course, you'll be able to process any kind of mail that comes into the mail room.

3. In this part of the training, you'll learn to recognize the differences between special mail and regular mail.

Determine which of the enabling objectives you should address first, which second, etc. When you've finished, you'll have the detailed sequence of the unit. Review your Strategy Checklist for those items requiring special emphasis, and decide how you'll handle their presentation. Then you'll have all of your practice, demonstration, and unit test items marked in the sequence of presentation, and you will have noted any that require special attention. It would be a good idea at this point to read all the demonstration items, in the sequence you've marked, to determine the flow of the material.

If the unit is long or complex, you may find it useful to outline it, using short statements of content. The first unit in most job training usually deals in a simple, straightforward manner with the input or condition with which the trainees will have to work. If this is the case with your material, you probably won't need an outline.

Here is a summary of the highlights to keep in mind when you're developing your introductory unit:

1. Write the instructor's materials to tell the instructor precisely what to do. The instructor may paraphrase the statements in the unit, or may learn them by heart. It's easier for the instructors to put the statements into words with which they are most comfortable.

2. Assume that the person who is to teach the course is qualified as an instructor.

3. Select your words carefully, keeping the trainees in mind, so you use language they'll understand and with which they'll feel comfortable.

4. Make each segment of the material as simple as possible, proceeding from the general to the specific, and the simple to the complex.

5. Use job aids and visual displays where they enhance trainee understanding and performance.

6. Avoid unnecessary paper. The instructor's materials should include only those job aids and visuals necessary for the instructor to deliver the learning to the trainees.

The opening of the first unit of the instructor's materials should begin with a simple statement that won't alarm or overwhelm the trainees. It develops the instruction at a moderate pace, indicating frequent checkpoints where the instructor is cautioned to make sure the trainees follow and understand the material. You need to build into the instructor's materials the capacity to assess trainee progress and adjust the pace accordingly. An experienced instructor usually will be able to determine how well the class is progressing and will adjust the progress of the instruction to the needs of the trainees.

The initial part of the unit leads to the first demonstration item. Be certain you have included all the necessary material for the enabling objectives before starting the first demonstration. For example, any new terms to be used in the demonstration should be introduced first.

If the first unit consists of several tasks or steps, you should go through each one separately, demonstrate and explain every activity the trainees will have to perform, and pause frequently to confirm that they understand. After you've completed a series of demonstrations, ask the trainees to practice what they have learned.

You'll determine the point at which to introduce practice by the complexity and importance of the activity. For example, there's little point in practicing a simple entry on a form unless it is in a context that's meaningful to the trainees. It's better to include several items that have meaning when performed together. Follow the same procedures you used for developing the demonstration items.

The guiding principle is to:

- Demonstrate.

- Have the trainees practice.

- Provide feedback.

You may need to repeat the demonstration and practice to be sure the trainees can perform the activities.

Your guidance should inform the instructor not to proceed until all trainees have demonstrated that they can perform the practice exercises correctly. There may be instances where you'll be able to permit slower learners to practice more without slowing the rest of the group. If you'll want that feature in your training, you'll need to plan for it at this stage of course development.

This chapter contains examples of the kinds of materials commonly used for practice exercises. Examples of practice exercises use three different instructional modes: instructor-led, slide-tape, and programmed instruction.

The remainder of the unit presentation follows the same pattern. Repeat the process for each demonstration and practice item that you've identified until you've satisfied all the requirements.

After you've done all that, read over the unit and ask yourself these questions:

1. Is the material clear, complete, and consistent throughout, including directions for the instructor?

2. Have you provided the necessary visuals and aids?

3. Is the unit length appropriate to the complexity and importance of the material?

Say: Now you will practice what you've learned. There are several pieces of mail in front of you. They're similar to those you'll be processing on the job. Your first task is to sort out all the Special Delivery mail.

Do: Allow the trainees enough time to sort through the mail. Then follow up by checking the individual stacks. If there are errors, reshuffle the mail and ask the trainee to sort it again. Answer any questions the trainee may have.

Say: Now sort the remaining pieces of mail. You should have stacks of certified, registered, air, and regular mail.

Do: When the trainees have finished, check the stacks. Reshuffle as above if necessary. Answer any questions the trainee may ask.

Say: Now we'll practice adding the correct Zip Codes. Go through each stack of mail and remove those pieces of mail that need to be corrected.

```
┌─────────────────┐
│                 │
│      20014      │
│                 │
└─────────────────┘
```

Slide 1

Narrator: This is a Zip Code. It's made up of five numbers. All Zip Codes have five numbers.

```
┌─────────────────┐
│                 │
│      1602       │
│                 │
└─────────────────┘
```

Slide 2

Narrator: Is this a correct Zip Code?

Why?

Write your answer on page 4 of your workbook.

PAUSE

No; 1602 is not a correct Zip Code because it doesn't have five numbers, or digits.

```
┌───────────┐
│           │
│   01026   │
│           │
│    930    │
│           │
│   0000    │
│           │
│   12182   │
│           │
└───────────┘
```

Slide 3

Choose the numbers that are correct Zip Codes and write them on page 5 of your workbook.

PAUSE

You should have written 01026 and 12182.

The presentation continues in this vein until all the material has been covered.

In this lesson you'll learn about Zip Codes and how to use a Zip Code Directory.

1. A Zip Code is made up of 5 numbers.

These could all be Zip Codes:
12345, 87654, 22222

Circle below the numbers that could be correct Zip Codes:

7284   20000

26312   593

89   55222

Now turn the page and check your answer.

ANSWERS TO PROGRAMMED INSTRUCTION EXAMPLE

Answers to Question 1:

26312
20000
55222

These are the only numbers containing five digits. The others cannot be Zip Codes, according to the definition on the previous page.

If you did not answer correctly, return to the previous page and make the corrections; then turn to page 28 and continue the lesson.

2. All outgoing domestic mail must have five-number Zip Codes. Mark the addresses below that must be corrected before being sent out.

John H. Doe
863 Elm Street
New York 19, NY

Mary Ellen Messanger
90019 Applewood
Apt. 6
Topeka, KS   30001

Mr. & Mrs. Elwood Conway
19 Reynolds Place
Farmington, VA   2631

Kenny Helpen
202 Harbor Drive
Tsausus, MO

Little & Small, Inc.
Half & Half Road
Nearly, Ark.   82103

When you've finished, check your work and turn the page for the correct answers.

If you answered no to any of the questions on page 54, make the adjustments required to correct the materials.

The next step is to administer the unit test. Instructions for test administration should state exactly what is expected. For example:

> We're going to have a test on what we just covered. Use your job description and your aids during the test. Before we begin, are there any questions?
>
> (Instructor answers any questions.)
>
> Turn to the Unit 2 test in your workbook. Follow the instructions to process the outgoing mail you see in front of you. Go ahead, unless there are questions.
>
> (As the trainees proceed, ensure that each step of the task is performed correctly. If there are errors, repeat the steps with each trainee until they all complete the process.)

Some units won't require any test. The need for a unit test is determined by the nature of the material. If, for example, the material is simple, well practiced, and to be used in the next unit, you probably don't need a test in this unit. Perhaps you can include the necessary performance in the next unit. Sometimes you risk disrupting the flow of material by interjecting an unnecessary test. On the other hand, tests provide an additional learning experience that may enhance the trainee's ability to proceed to the next training unit. The decision whether or not to test is an individual one based on your own good judgment.

The usual procedure is to demonstrate, practice, provide feedback, test, and provide feedback again. The key element of the practice and test sessions is the *feedback*. If trainees learn the results of their actions, they may correct their mistakes and perform correctly. Without feedback, they may continue to repeat their errors. Every test should be reviewed immediately after its completion so the instructor can provide the trainees with the essential feedback.

Remember, *tests are part of the learning process.*

After you've completed the first unit, check it once more before proceeding to the next unit.

Write the remainder of the units by repeating every step in the development process.

It's important to review the entire job in the final unit, with a comprehensive demonstration, followed by exercises that cover the course's entire contents. The final practice may repeat some parts of the materials covered in earlier units. Up to this point, the materials have explained segments of the job to the trainees. This final review exercise enables the trainees to understand and practice the job in its entirety, with emphasis on the sequence of tasks. When the review is completed, be sure to include the resources necessary to answer any trainee's questions before beginning the final exercise.

PREPARE CRITERION EXERCISE AND TEST

The course criterion test is used for developmental purposes and should be kept in that form throughout the testing of the course itself. When the course is finally tested and ready to be released for use in the field, it may have to be modified as a final test.

A course criterion exercise (or final exercise) is necessary to ensure completeness. This exercise is handled just like the unit exercises, with the primary difference being that it covers the entire course. The criterion exercise may be a separate exercise or may be included as the final unit exercise. It is, in effect, a dress rehearsal for the course criterion test. As in the unit exercises, feedback should be provided immediately upon completion.

PREPARE TRAINEE'S MATERIALS

When you're satisfied that the instructor's materials are complete, you're ready to begin preparation of the trainee's materials. For the most part, you can derive the trainee's materials from the instructor's materials. As with the instructor's materials, avoid unnecessary paper in preparing the trainee's materials. Include only those items that will be used in the course.

The trainee's materials should contain statements of objectives, copies of the exercises, and copies of the test items. If some of the visuals used in the course will be useful as aids, include reproductions of them.

You may be tempted to include in the trainee's materials all related information for on-the-job use as reference materials. Experience has proven that trainees rarely refer to the materials after the course is completed unless the training materials are also job procedure manuals containing essential references. Therefore, it's usually expensive and wasteful to try to use the trainee's materials as anything except an aid to course presentation and learning.

You may, for any number of reasons, not wish to distribute all the trainee's materials at the same time. It's perfectly acceptable to give the trainees the materials as they're needed. However, you should keep in mind the logistics and the potential class disruption involved when you provide the materials to the trainees piecemeal.

PREPARE VISUALS

You should now prepare the required visual aids, keeping in mind the need for clarity, legibility, and ease of handling. There may be times when you'll have professional graphics support, but often you'll need to prepare your own visuals. If you have access to professional support, by all means take advantage of it. Be sure you build enough lead time into your schedule for the production and probable revision of the graphics materials.

The instructor's materials should tell the instructor what to show or use, and when. Make certain that your instructions don't call for too-frequent changing of visuals or for leaving them displayed after they've served their purpose.

Now, make sure the program works by trying it out on yourself, using the visuals or simulating their use. It's easy to confuse procedures when you're writing the materials—to have instructions calling for two slides projected at the same time, or the wrong slide at the wrong time. Going through the course and following your instructions is the surest way of discovering procedural errors.

When you've completed the instructor's and the trainee's materials, with the visuals, make a final check of the package by asking yourself:

1. Do all the instructor's materials track with the trainee's materials?

2. Are the visuals in the right places and do they show the right things?

3. Are the aids correct?

4. Will the instructor find the directions in the proper places?

By completing this final check, you may find special problems or additional points that should be covered at specific times during the course.

The trainee's materials will often include a glossary containing terms that may be new to the trainees or that require only brief review. Decide if you're going to include a glossary and, if so, write it now. It should be included as part of the instructor's materials, as well.

10

Task 8: Develop Instructor's or Administrator's Guide

The instructor's (or administrator's) guide provides any additional information needed by the instructor to prepare for and to administer the course. The guide should include:

1. Course Overview: A brief description stating what the course does—here, for example, the course teaches trainees how to process incoming and outgoing mail.

2. Course Length: Include total length and the times expected for each unit.

3. Instructor Preparation: What the instructor must know and do before teaching the course, including how to handle aids, rehearse the course, etc.

4. Trainee Prerequisites: A list of courses, knowledge, and experience the trainee must have prior to attending the training sessions.

5. Instructor/Trainee Ratio: The number of trainees assigned to each instructor.

6. Training Facilities, Equipment, and Materials: Detailed description to facilitate the work of the instructor and to help ensure that the required materials are present.

7. Adaptation Requirements: Pertains to courses being taught to several different divisions of the same organization or in different locations within the same organization. There may be variation in the types of inputs and in the conditions with which the trainees and the instructors must deal. This section should provide the instructor the means to make the course applicable to different locations or organizations. As a minimum, it should indicate which sections of the course are sensitive to changed locations or organizations, and offer guidance to the instructor.

8. Course Objectives: A list of what the trainees will have learned upon course completion. The objectives from the instructor's or trainee's materials may be used or simply referenced.

9. Plan of Instruction: Detailed description of the instructor's role, use of materials, aids, criterion test, glossaries, use of feedback, and suggested techniques.

It's important for all these items to be present in the instructor's guide. If you have any doubts, include too much information. Remember, this package may be used by people who have never seen it before.

**ASSEMBLE
ENTIRE PACKAGE**

After you've prepared the guide and the introduction, you'll have completed all the course materials, including:

1. Instructor's or administrator's guide.

2. Introduction and remainder of the instructor's materials.

3. Trainee's materials.

4. Visuals.

5. Aids, glossaries, and other special materials.

**REVISE AND
CONDUCT DRY
RUN**

Review the entire package carefully; look for inconsistencies and technical errors. When you're satisfied with the package, ask an associate to critique the materials. If you encourage an honest critique, you'll benefit from having a fresh pair of eyes looking at your program. After all, by this time, you may have spent months preparing the course and may have difficulty perceiving it from a student's point of view.

Make your revisions after the reviews are completed.

Next, go through the course on a dry run, from beginning to end, with you acting as instructor. Ideally, you should find someone to play the part of a trainee.

You may be fortunate enough to have another person play the instructor, in which case, you should observe the instructor, the trainee, and their interactions. Be alert for weaknesses in the program that can be fixed before the next stage of testing. When the training session is over, you should encourage the instructor and the trainee to criticize the materials and to assess whether, and how well, the objectives were met. Ask them to make suggestions for improving the program. If the instructor and the trainees participating in the dry run are typical of the larger population for whom the training was developed, it will be to your advantage to pay close attention to their comments.

Make any changes you consider necessary, and when you're satisfied with the package, proceed to Task 9.

11

Task 9: Try Out Training Package

The desk review is the first systematic tryout of the entire training package. It's performed by the training developer and others who may have testing responsibilities. The desk review requires each reviewer, individually, to review the material critically to determine if the package is complete, trainable, technically correct, and consistent with the standards of the organization. This review generally leads to revisions. When the revisions are completed, the package is reviewed again to ensure that the recommended changes have all been accounted for. The package is then prepared for the developmental test.

PERFORM DESK REVIEW

The developmental test is performed on subjects who meet the basic qualifications to take the course. They are "simulated" trainees who provide the instructor practice in presentation. It's also a good opportunity to test the legibility and utility of the visual material, the practice and test items, and the other administrative details of the course. The technical content of the course will, for the most part, have been verified prior to this phase of testing.

PERFORM DEVELOPMENTAL TEST

This test is a dress rehearsal. The procedures that are modified as a result will be included in the course material and presented in the new form during the field tryout.

**PERFORM FIELD
TRYOUT**

The field tryout is designed to prepare an instructor in the field to train others. This tryout is performed in a similar way to the developmental test. The person who developed the training package will often have the responsibility for providing the initial field presentations.

12

Task 10: Analyze Results and Revise

The field tryout is the final stage of testing of the training package. The data collected during this tryout tell you what shortcomings exist in the course materials or in the course administration. These data are carefully reviewed by the same group that has been involved in all the testing, and decisions are made regarding any revisions. The changes are then incorporated into the package and submitted for final review.

When you finally release the training program for general use by the people who need it, you shouldn't try to hide your feelings of satisfaction and accomplishment.

Training is a discipline fraught with uncertainty. You frequently don't know ahead of time what level of motivation the trainees will bring, or what you might do on purpose to enhance, or by accident, to diminish that eagerness or willingness to become a productive participant in the program.

If 75 to 90 percent of the trainees meet the objectives, you've done an excellent job. If performance falls consistently below that level, you should take another look at the program and search for methods to improve the results.

KEEPING THE PROGRAM ALIVE

Be sure, at the time you turn over the program for someone else to administer, that there is a method to keep the program up-to-date. One of the greatest failings of many training programs is that they become obsolete because resources were not made available to maintain and update them. The world changes, and the training related to that world must keep pace.

**USING THE
PROCESS**

The material you've covered to this point covers the basic *process* of training development. The remainder of the text contains information that you'll find useful under different circumstances. If you follow the basic process as it has been defined in Part 2 of this Guide, you should be able to produce usable training materials that meet their objectives.

As you use the process and become comfortable with its details, you can expect your products to improve. You should discuss the process with your colleagues so you can adapt it to fit your needs more precisely.

Use the process to develop your training and to monitor the work of others. Evolve the methodology to suit your needs, but take care to preserve the basic concepts and rationale on which the process is based.

13

Exercises

The following exercises have been designed for those who want to try the techniques and practices described in this Guide. The exercises can be useful to the student in a class or to a professional working alone. In many cases there are no "correct" answers—some may be better than others, but the individual situation may be more important than any dogma set forth in a text of this type. Discussions with co-workers can often lead to the most satisfactory decisions regarding the development of the training. Always be prepared to discuss your work openly with others and be ready to accept valid criticism and input. Your product usually will be the better for it.

The exercises follow the same sequence as the chapters in the book.

A. Prepare a brief plan to develop a training sequence that includes both positive and negative reinforcement.
B. Show how you would account for individual differences in your plan for (A) above.
C. Explain how the students' motivation might alter your approach. Give examples of motivational elements of the training.
D. Describe how you can build the training so that all the trainees

are guaranteed 100 percent scores on their final performance test.

EXERCISE 2

A. Write a job description for which you will later develop a training program. Select a relatively simple job, one that has no more than five tasks.
B. Draw a diagram of the job, task by task.
C. Identify the training requirements for the job. Use the Training Requirements Form. State your assumptions about the target population.

EXERCISE 3

A. Review the Examples of Course Objectives in Chapter 2 of the text. Rewrite the "good" ones to make them better.
B. Write the objectives for the first task of the job you've defined.
C. Review your objectives. Rewrite them to improve them. If possible, review them with a co-worker and revise them again.

EXERCISE 4

Examine your objectives and the task descriptions to determine the enabling objectives. Write them down and proceed as in Exercise 3.

EXERCISE 5

A. Develop your course criterion test items from the objectives you've developed.
B. Check and recheck to ensure there is at least one criterion test item for each objective. Complete the Criterion Test Item Log in Chapter 4.
C. Review your work with an associate and revise as required.

EXERCISE 6

A. Select one of the tasks in the job you've defined and develop your demonstration items. Select the method of demonstration with which you feel most comfortable.
B. Using the demonstration items you developed, prepare a set of practice items to match them.
C. Develop test items from the demonstration and practice items you just prepared.
D. Review and revise the demonstration, practice, and test items until you're satisfied that they'll do the job.

EXERCISE 7

A. Complete the Strategy Checklist in Chapter 6 of the text.
B. Review and discuss your decisions and the rationale you used to reach your conclusions. Be prepared to modify any of your choices if you become convinced that there may be a better way to reach the objectives.

A. Prepare the instructor's materials—Course Introduction, based on your strategy.

B. Prepare the instructor's materials for training and testing of the first task (first unit), following the strategy and using the material you've developed thus far.

C. Review and revise the instructor's materials until you're satisfied with them.

D. Prepare the materials in another format, using different media. Repeat (C).

EXERCISE 8

Repeat Exercise 8 for developing the trainee's materials.

EXERCISE 9

A. Prepare a glossary for the materials you produced.

B. Ask an associate to review the glossary and revise as necessary. (If a great number of terms are in your glossary, perhaps you've used too much jargon or too many technical terms.)

EXERCISE 10

A. Prepare an instructor's or administrator's guide suitable for use with the materials you've already developed.

B. Review all the materials you've prepared to this point to make certain that they all fit together and that the objectives have a high probability of being achieved by use of the materials. Revise as necessary.

EXERCISE 11

A. Try the training package on actual students to determine if it works and where it needs fixing.

B. Revise the materials and test them again.

C. Repeat (B) until you're satisfied the objectives can be met using this package with the target population.

EXERCISE 12

BEYOND THE BASIC PROCESS | Part 3

14

Workshops and Conferences

Planning a conference or workshop, especially one that will be held at a location other than the usual work place, requires considerable care and effort. If the workshop activities appear to the participants to be well organized and smoothly run, the aura of confidence will make the trainees more comfortable and probably enhance the learning. Most of the preparations for workshops in this section are administrative—you'll use the same process for developing the training materials you use for any other kind of training. First, let's look at some of the decisions that need to be made.

Instructors

Ensure that instructors are available who are knowledgeable in all areas of the training to be presented.

Duration of the Training

When deciding on the duration of the workshop, keep in mind that:

- Too much material tends to make learning superficial.
- Too little material wastes training time.

Participants

Determine whether:

- The group is being trained as remediation.
- It is a high potential group being nurtured to assume greater responsibilities and higher positions.

Select participants.

- Highly technical or complex training requires more instructors per student and a stricter selection process.
- Selection of participants could be by:
  - Nomination by supervisors. All supervisors should have a common understanding of the meeting objectives and the qualities desired in the participants.
  - If the number of participants is unlimited, selection could be strictly on a volunteer basis.

Selection of a Training Site

If the workshop is to be held away from the usual work place, consider the following:

- Number of participants.
- Availability of funding for travel, accommodations, meals, etc.
- Suitability of conference facilities.
- Costs for conference rooms, accessibility, lighting, set-up, size, etc.
- Availability of breakout rooms for discussion groups and evening sessions.
- Accessibility to public transportation.
- Transportation to and from terminals.
- Availability of recreational facilities at conference site.

- Availability of transportation for local touring and recreational side trips.

- Adequacy of food service to meet the group requirements.

- Availability of a photographer.

- Banquet facilities.

Complete the Conference Facility Checklist found on the following pages.

1. Cost of rooms.

2. Daily cost of meals:
   a. How are individual charges accounted for?
   b. If participants skip meals, will there still be a charge?
   c. What other eating facilities are in the area?

3. Menus.
   a. Are menus available for all meals?
   b. Are choices available at meals?
   c. Can participants request special dietary meals, such as sugar-free or salt-free?
   d. Can participants "upgrade" and have beverage service at their own expense?

4. How do participants get to and from the site?

5. What recreational facilities are available for use in the off hours?

6. Are brochures available showing rooms, facilities, etc.?

7. Will the participants be allowed to remain for additional time at the same rates?

8. How much advance notice is required for room cancellations?

9. How are no-shows handled?

10. What medical facilities are available?

11. How do we arrange reception for arriving participants?

12. How do we establish an open or a cash bar?
    a. Costs?
    b. Restrictions?

13. What arrangements are required for evening sessions?

14. What facilities are in the area for participants' after-hours activities?

15. Conference facilities.
    _____ Large meeting room.
    _____ Breakout rooms.
    _____ Morning and afternoon coffee breaks.
    _____ Overhead projectors.
    _____ 16mm film projectors.
    _____ 35mm slide projectors.
    _____ Projection screen.
    _____ Chalkboards and flip chart paper/stands.
    _____ Videotape recorders/players.
    _____ Audiotape recorders/players.
    _____ Video/TV monitors.
    _____ Photographer.

16. What is the usual dress for participants at this time of year? Do people usually dress for dinner?

17. Are car rentals available?

18. Is there anything we should alert the participants to bring or to be prepared for?

19. Who will be our contact?
    a. Name?
    b. Phone?

20. What are the payment arrangements?

21. Will the establishment provide any gratis or reduced rate rooms or meals for our staff?

22. Are there facilities for the handicapped, such as wheelchairs?

23. Are typing and duplication facilities available? If so, how can we use them?
    a. Cost?
    b. Limitations?

24. Do conferences sometimes break during the day for recreation and then reconvene for late sessions?

25. Are there special times when we must be out of the meeting rooms so they can be cleaned, etc.? If so, when?

ADDITIONAL NOTES

Assigning Staff

Assign an appropriate number of instructors.

Assign sufficient administrative support, including someone who is able to assume responsibility for detail and who is available to remain at the conference site throughout the program.

Getting Materials

Based on your analysis of the organization's needs, collect and develop appropriate materials. Articles or exercises may be purchased.

- Articles in the public domain may be adapted to fit this organization. Job titles, department names, etc., may be changed, but the original source should be noted.

- Films are available from many sources, including the Library of Congress and other libraries.

Informing the Participants

- Obtain a list of the attendees and their addresses.

- Contact participants at least one month before the workshop, if possible.

- Send letters to participants, congratulating them for having been selected for the workshop. The sample letter on the next page includes many informational items that may or may not be relevant to your workshop. Try to include answers to questions you might ask if you were attending a workshop for a week at some unfamiliar location, a long distance from your home.

(The letter should be sent on official stationery, and should be signed by the program coordinator.)

Dear _____:

Congratulations on having been selected to attend the XYZ Workshop at the Dew Drop Inn near Wetfoot, Oregon.

We've designed a busy and interesting week for you and we're looking forward to getting acquainted with you and sharing an eventful five days.

Unless you're driving to the conference, transportation from any of the area airports, train, or bus stations will be arranged for you. The distance from the terminals is about 60 miles. The conference center has vehicles that will pick you up and deliver you to the hotel for $10 per person. You are requested to arrive in the area between 4 and 6 P.M. on the Sunday preceding the conference. If you could arrange your schedule to fit into that time frame, it would make transportation simpler.

The conference will be ending at about 1 P.M. on Friday. You should arrange return transportation to arrive at the terminal about 4 P.M. Again, the conference center will provide transportation to the stations and airports for the same charge.

Just to set your mind at ease about the conference, here are some things you might like to know:

The conference is scheduled to begin on an informal note Sunday evening, when we'll have a little get together so everyone can say hello and meet the other folks who'll be spending the week together.

The Monday through Friday schedule is approximately 8:30 A.M. to 5:00 P.M., with a fairly long lunch break. There are optional evening activities both for work and for recreation.

The site has indoor and outdoor swimming pools, and tennis courts. A public golf course is nearby. A National Park is about five minutes away, and the country-side offers spectacular scenery. There are no car rental facilities nearby, but transportation can be arranged if several people want to go somewhere in the evening.

Dress is casual during the day and in the evening. There is no need for any semblance of formality.

You are expected to attend the scheduled banquet on Thursday evening.

If you decide to remain beyond the conference, we have arranged reduced rates for you. Several brochures of the area are enclosed.

Meal service at the conference facility is excellent. Sample menus are enclosed. If you have any special dietary needs, please be sure to make note of them on the attached form and return it immediately.

If, for any reason, you will not be able to attend as planned, please call reception desk at (111)555-5555 to arrange for a cancellation. We have enclosed a list of scheduled attendees and their addresses.

If you have any questions, call or write and we'll try to get the answers for you. We're all looking forward to seeing you at the conference.

Sincerely,

J. J. Jones, Conference Coordinator

Name _____

Organization _____

If you are coming to the conference by air, train, or bus, please complete the following:

I will be arriving on (circle one)
Flight/Train/Bus at _____ terminal.

I will arrive at _____
My scheduled departure is from _____ at _____
o'clock on _____

Are there any special arrangements we should make for you?
___ Yes ___ No. Please describe _____
_____
_____

What name do you use at work? _____

How do you prefer to be addressed informally? _____

How do you like your name to appear on official documents? _____
_____

What else should we know about you to make you more comfortable? _____
_____
_____

Materials Preparation

Allow sufficient time for printing of the materials and for ordering special supplies. You need to find out how much lead time is required for:

- Printing workbooks.
- Special printing, such as silk-screened notebook covers, special tabs, etc.
- Certificate holders, or other presentations.

You should also:

- Prepare an identification badge for each participant to wear at the first get together.
- Prepare a nameplate for each participant's place at the conference table so instructors and students can easily identify participants. Writing the names on both sides of the nameplate aids identification.
- Make sure you have enough materials for all participants, instructors, and observers. It's a good idea to plan for two or three extras.

Conference Site Preparations

As soon as possible, provide the conference site with the following information:

- List of participants.
- Participants' travel plans, such as:
  Name of carrier.
  Number of flight, train, bus, etc.
  Arrival time.
  Terminal.
- Participants' departure details, preferably at least two days before the end of the workshop.

Once at the conference site, don't assume that the establishment will follow your instructions exactly. It's always a good idea to follow up.

Cash Bars

- Notify establishment if and when you'll require a cash bar.

- Notify establishment if you want snacks or hors d'oeuvres served.

- Make sure establishment has correct days and times for cash bars. Follow up after arrangements have been made.

Banquet

- Decide on the day and times for the banquet, entertainment, and any bar service for a specified number of people.

- Obtain main course entree choices.

- Make sure an extra table is set up with a tablecloth for display purposes for awards, photos, or other items.

- If there are to be banquet speakers:

    Find out if they require a podium, or whether they will speak from the table.

    Inform the establishment sufficiently far in advance if a sleeping room is required for the guest speaker (to guarantee that one will be available).

Administrative Duties at the Workshop

Arrive at least two hours before the start of the first get together and make sure the following matters have been taken care of:

- Ensure the conference room has been set up according to your instructions.

- Be sure you have adequate supplies of items such as:
    Workbooks.
    Tablets and sharpened pencils.
    Chalk and other writing and drawing devices.
    Cellophane and masking tapes.
    Stapler.
    Certificates of course completion.
    Name tags for conference table.
    Badges for initial sessions.
    Pencil sharpener.

AT THE
WORKSHOP OR
CONFERENCE

Three-hole punch.
Typewriter and supplies.
Glue or paste.
Paper cutter.
Conference critique forms for participants to complete.

- Put name cards, workbooks, tablets, pencils, etc. around conference tables.

- Have a sign placed in a conspicuous location to guide participants to the initial get together.

- Confirm that all participants are present or accounted for.

During the Conference

Apart from dealing with minor crises, attend to the following:

- Keep participants and the establishment informed of schedules and any changes.

- Make any special arrangements that instructors may require, for example, lunch served in a conference room for a special session.

- If you're going to have photos, plan for the photographer to take group pictures so copies will be available before the end of the conference.

- Inform the photographer of the banquet schedule if you want photographs of that event.

- Survey the participants to determine their interest in social activities. Arrange transportation for evening activities.

- If the establishment provides transportation for field trips or tours, make sure they are aware of your needs.

- Select the banquet menu.

- If there will be lunch sessions, obtain menus for distribution to participants approximately one hour before lunch is to be served.

- If certificates are presented at the banquet, be sure they're ready at the time of the banquet. Participants generally appreciate receiving their awards and certificates prior to leaving the conference.

Checking Out

- Determine the correct checkout procedure, such as times and whether participants may have lunch before leaving.

- Determine the times that transportation will leave for the terminals and inform participants.

- Ensure that participants understand the checkout procedures.

Consider a follow-up get together or mailing to reinforce or consolidate the participants' ideas about their training. Mail any special materials or information that may have been promised to the participants.

FOLLOW-UP

15

Administration Guide for Self-Instructional Training

Self-administered, learner-managed, or self-instructional training is, simply, that training in which the learner, student, or trainee determines which lessons to work and when to perform them. The term self-paced is often used, erroneously, to be synonymous with self-administered. Self-administered training is, of course, also self-paced, but self-paced training may be accomplished in a classroom where there are an instructor and other trainees. Self-paced means only that each trainee proceeds at a pace that's comfortable for that individual.

A correspondence course is a familiar example of self-administered training. Self-administered training may be performed on the job, at home, in a learning laboratory, or any place that's conducive to learning.

This mode of training may use several types of media, or only one, depending on the needs of the program, the subject matter, and learner preferences and motivation.

A number of advantages and disadvantages are inherent in self-administered training. The primary advantage is the low administrative cost, compared with the cost of classrooms and transporta-

DEFINITION OF SELF-ADMINISTERED TRAINING

91

tion of learners to a central location. Many people feel that they learn better and easier if they can control the times, place, and duration of their training. On the other hand, the disadvantages include greater development costs because of the need to package the materials completely, and the necessity for a different and higher level of motivation to learn. If the self-administered training is an option the learner can choose, then the additional cost of developing two versions of the same program is another disadvantage.

The overriding factor influencing the decisions relative to self-administered training are logistical, primarily cost.

For example, if there is need to train many people in locations throughout the world, there may be no question that the correct choice is self-administered training, even if the materials require translation into several languages.

If the training is for a high turnover job, the self-administered choice may be the correct one, especially if only a few people at a time are ready for or need the training.

Self-administered training may also be a good choice when the subject matter is relatively unchanging or when the course materials are easily changed.

The following example of self-instructional training presents the beginning of a course in word processing.

Background

Most people beginning to learn word processing have no prior experience with computers and are often unaware that word processing systems are computer based. Often, they experience considerable anxiety and apprehension, based on the fear of computers and, even more important, the neophytes' fear that they might damage the machine by doing something stupid.

The Training Model

It's most important that the anxiety be allayed. The following kinds of statements in the initial training segments help make the trainee more comfortable and ready to begin learning.

> In the next few days you'll be learning what this powerful new tool is and how to use it.

> An instructor won't be standing in front of the class lecturing you on the use of this system. You'll be *reading* and *doing*. It's most important that you read everything in this document as you proceed. The instructions are clear and easy to follow.

This workbook is yours to keep. It's yours during the training and it's yours when you get back to your job where you can use it as a reference.

Write in the workbook. Make notes of things you want to remember. Underline as you see fit. The workbook is a tool for your personal use.

Remember, nobody's looking over your shoulder, nor is anyone timing you. Work at a pace that's comfortable for you so you'll be sure you can complete the exercises.

We call this training *hands on* because you'll be spending most of your time working directly with the equipment.

You've probably already been away from the machine longer reading this lesson than you'll be for the rest of the training. Before you leave today, you'll begin to feel comfortable with this new system.

Just a word before you begin the first exercise. Many people have never been exposed to a system like this before and are a little (or even a lot) apprehensive about becoming involved with a computer.

That's right; in case you didn't know it, this word processor is a computer system.

But don't let that bother you if you're unfamiliar with computers. Just remember to think of it as a *tool* that will help you do your work better and faster than ever before. You'll be its master; not the other way around. You'll see how easy it is once you get into it.

In this lesson you're going to become familiar with the equipment, and you'll begin to learn how to use it.

It probably looks a little different to you from other office equipment you've used, but don't let that frighten you. It's really not difficult to learn how to use this equipment.

Before we get into the use of the system, let's take a few minutes to learn about the different pieces of equipment in front of you.

First, there's a keyboard. You can see it's pretty much like keyboards on typewriters, with some differences you'll learn about as we continue.

Press some of the keys to get the feel of the keyboard. You won't see anything on the screen because the system isn't ready to accept your inputs yet. You're just getting the feel of the keyboard.

You don't need to know how to type to use this system; but if you've ever typed before, you'll notice that the keys feel somewhat different from other machines.

Try pressing the keys ever so gently so they make no sound. It isn't necessary to press the keys very hard to get the system to accept your inputs. You can try again later, when the system is running.

Now look at the screen. . . .

The introductory session proceeds through each piece of equipment, describing its function and allowing the trainee to touch and use each part. This process is followed until the equipment is turned on and ready to accept input. A sample of an instructional sequence from the beginning of the training follows:

> . . . If you pressed the RETURN key, you created a new paragraph, with extra space between the lines.
>
> If you skipped a line, you're like most other people. You pressed the RETURN key to get to the next line. That's perfectly logical. You were asked to type your name and address just as you would on any other keyboard. Who could blame you for pressing the RETURN key?
>
> The important thing to remember is that the RETURN key in this system creates a new paragraph. One way to get to the next line without creating a new paragraph is to continue keying words. The system recognizes the right margin and automatically begins the next line. Try it. . . .

The training proceeds through the basic operations, one at a time, permitting the trainees to master each operation before moving on. Practice exercises are included to provide feedback to the trainees and to establish confidence in their performance.

More complex and advanced operations are added in the context of the trainees' jobs. The training asks the trainees to perform an activity similar to one that might be performed in their own jobs. If the trainees prefer not to invent applications, the materials provide optional exercises.

An example of more advanced material follows:

> The SUBSTITUTE option allows you to change any passage automatically (single word or small group of words). Here's how it works.
>
> Let's say, for example, you want to change *Jon* to *John* throughout an entire document. The name Jon appears many times in the document.
>
> Here's what you'd do (don't do it yet):
>
> • Get the "A" menu.
>
> • Select the "S" for SUBSTITUTE.
>
> • Scroll to the beginning of the document.
>
> • In the first set of brackets, type Jon.
>
> • In the second set of brackets, type John.
>
> • When you're certain you've typed the terms correctly, press RETURN.
>
> • Each time Jon appears, type "Y" if you want to change it. If you don't want to change it, type "N" to continue.
>
> If you want all appearances to be changed automatically (without asking you if it's OK), type ALL after you type John.

Each of the functions is presented and the trainee is asked to perform them, building the skill and knowledge required to become proficient in the use of the word processor.

Background

The objectives of knowledge training are demonstrations by the trainees that they can perform specific activities to criteria—the same kind of objective found for skills training. For example, if the training developer wants the trainees to learn the poem *Hiawatha,* the objective should be that the trainee demonstrate the ability to recite (or write) the first three stanzas, without error.

If the objective is written for demonstration of the knowledge, the training is more likely to accomplish the ends than if the objective were stated in terms such as, "... the trainee will understand the poem ...."

The Training Model

As in skills training, knowledge training follows the pattern of demonstration, practice, and test. The demonstration often takes the form of a classroom lecture, audiovisual presentation, reading, or participation in a discussion group.

The practice phase may take the form of recitation, writing, analysis, or study group activity. Often the old standby, drill and practice, may be the best method for knowledge that must be learned by rote. However, drill and practice may be an excellent method for practicing the multiplication tables, but may be less effective for practicing cost accounting procedures.

Testing is best accomplished where the trainee can demonstrate proficiency with the material, via performance. Performance may take the form of reciting the poem before the class. If the class is large and if all trainees have the same assignment, such recitation could be very time consuming. Recitation by a small number of trainees selected at random might prove valuable because all trainees should be prepared, and some additional learning will occur if they listen to the recitations of the others.

Testing of facts by true/false and multiple-choice tests is another method traditionally used because the answers to the items can be scored easily, either by hand or by a machine. There is little question that this kind of testing is advantageous for administrative purposes. But a completion test may be as objective, while more cumbersome to administer and score. Asking a trainee to write the first line of the second stanza is a far more reliable measure of the trainee's knowl-

EXAMPLE OF KNOWLEDGE TRAINING— PROCUREMENT IN THE FEDERAL GOVERNMENT

edge than asking the trainee to select the correct line from four choices. Even a less reliable indicator of learning is to present the trainee with a line in a true/false question.

The point is that the objective of the training is to impart learning. A training objective should never be oriented toward student failure. Therefore, tests should be considered part of the learning process and constructed so that the trainee receives feedback in a form usable to correct performance. A training designer is not interested in determining only whether or not the trainee can meet the training objectives, the training designer's professional objective is to *ensure* that the trainee is able to perform.

The basic model for knowledge training is essentially the same as for skills training; only the methods may vary. The demonstration, practice, and test aspects of the training design should be constructed so that they are iterative, continuing until the objectives are reached, as illustrated.

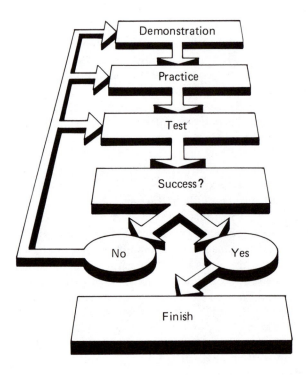

On the following pages you'll find a sample from a knowledge training program.

SAMPLE FROM A KNOWLEDGE TRAINING PROGRAM

This excerpt is adapted from a four-day program to train executives in the principles and operations of contracting and procurement in the federal government. The sample is taken from the instructor's manual lesson plan.

LESSON PLAN—DAY 3

If you didn't complete the activities scheduled for Day 2, do so before beginning the Day 3 work.

When you've completed the Day 2 activities, summarize the procurement process. Emphasis should be on the process rather than the details of the case. Your summary should include these points:

- Determination of the need for services.
- Definition of the needs.
- Search for potential suppliers of the service.
- Preparation of an Invitation for Bid (IFB).
- Establishment of critera for selection.
- Analysis of proposals.
- Preliminary decisions.
- Follow-up evaluation.
- Negotiation.
- Final decision.

Before proceeding to the next topic, answer any questions the students may have about the Day 2 activities.

Begin the Day 3 activities by telling the class, "This morning we're going to consider the remainder of this procurement, while making certain that the rest of the administrative workload can be completed satisfactorily. We're going to examine some techniques for planning and organizing the work." (Objective 6)

Now that the firm has been selected to perform the assessment of the condition of the electrical system, the managers are launched on a major activity, which they must monitor carefully, while attending to their myriad other duties and responsibilities. The manager needs to plan and organize the work to ensure that all the parts will receive the needed attention when required and with the necessary resources.

Ask the class, "What are the other tasks and activities the manager will need to accomplish to complete the job of refurbishing the plant's electrical system?"

Lead the class discussion, continuing to broaden the scope until the planned-for three-year program begins to take form. Write the activities on the chalkboard. These items should be included in the following list of activities noted by the class:

- Appoint a project monitor from the administrative staff.

- Meet with the contractor's representatives, including the project manager.

- Assist the contractor to start the project.

- Respond to needs of the contractor.

- Review contractor's progress reports.

- Meet with the contractor for progress reviews.

- Deal with emergency and extraordinary situations.

- Plan for next steps in the refurbishing program.

- Report the contractor's progress to higher management.

- Perform source search, IFB preparation, and source selection for the next phase of the refurbishing program.

- Schedule refurbishing contracts and procurements.

- Follow up each activity of the refurbishing.

- Inspect, review, and coordinate the contractor's activities.

- Keep plant personnel informed of the contractor's activities that might interfere with their daily operations.

- Perform inspections of materials, workmanship, and reports.

Lead a discussion about delegation of responsibility to staff. Include the legal limitations of delegation. The class should quickly become convinced that the administrative officer's workload is sufficiently heavy so that the additional burden of the refurbishing project would be impossible to handle personally. The class should become convinced in a matter of minutes, if not seconds, that delegation is required.

The mechanics of the delegation will require some further discussion, including:

- Differences between delegation and abdication.

- Degree of authority to go with the responsibilities.

- Limitations of delegation.

- Specification of the delegation—a detailed definition of what the responsibilities are.

- When to delegate and when to terminate the delegation.

- Reporting requirements.

Using the activities list you've put on the chalkboard, explain the use, value, and limitations of Gantt charting and PERT diagramming. Include the following points in your discussion:

- Preparation of any type of chart forces the user to think about the entire program and the relationships among the activities.

- The charts are a form of communication, informing others of precisely what is expected, and when.

- The charts give the manager a picture of the expected status at any point in the program.

- Maintenance of the charts can be time consuming, but each time a chart is updated, the manager's knowledge of the program status is updated.

- Performers and managers have the same understanding of the activities to be performed and when they are due for completion.

Describe how a Gantt chart is prepared.
Explain that this type of chart is also called a time-line or waterfall chart. The essential elements of this type of chart are:

- Activity title or description.

- Activities which typically require a period of time for completion. For example, "Appoint a manager" would not usually be found on a Gantt chart.

- Calendar time from start to finish of each activity.

- Level of labor resource to be applied.

- Cost information is rarely included.

Demonstrate the Gantt chart technique on the chalkboard using the first activity.
Answer any trainee questions about the technique.

Ask the groups to form again to prepare a Gantt chart for all the items listed on the chalkboard, and others they believe should be on the chart. Ask the trainees to limit the chart to the first twelve months of the program.

Allow time for them to copy the information from the chalkboard.

Request that they return to the class within thirty minutes. Remind each group after twenty minutes.

When you reconvene the class, ask one of the students to act as scribe at the flipchart and proceed to build a Gantt chart, using the inputs from each group.

If there are questionable entries or some that require explanation, ask the submitting group to explain. Encourage challenges to any of the inputs and to any of the items written on the chalkboard.

Lead a discussion about the merits and shortcomings of this kind of management tool. Encourage criticism of the technique and then encourage defense of it. Your objective is to ensure trainees' understanding and their ability to use the technique.

Explain, briefly, the concept of PERT-type of planning tools. Begin by explaining that PERT is the acronym for *P*rogram *E*valuation *R*eview *T*echnique, and was developed in the '50s for use in the Navy nuclear submarine construction program. The concepts to convey are:

- Critical path.

- Relationships among the variables and activities.

- *Related to time.*

- Tied to costs.

Maintenance of a manual system can be extremely difficult, therefore the technique is of little value in many settings because there are no resources to continually revise the complex diagrams. However, computer-generated diagrams make the technique extremely valuable.

Demonstrate the technique using the chalkboard and laying out the critical path, with assistance from the class. Do only three or four activities and/or events, then stop and ask the groups to form again and complete the diagram *for the first year only.* Allow about thirty minutes for the groups to complete their work.

Reconvene the class and repeat the process used for the Gantt chart, having a student draw the PERT diagram on the chalkboard.

Discuss the positive and negative aspects of the process and its application to projects of this type. Encourage questions and class participation in the discussion. Emphasize that perhaps the most useful aspect of PERT is the graphic representation of the many dependencies that assists planning and optimizes the allocation of resources to get the job done. It is particularly useful in construction programs.

After the groups have completed the planning processes and have the Gantt and PERT charts in hand, ask the trainees to read *Electrical Modernization— Part 3* in their workbooks.

Lead a discussion of the decision-making process used by the trainees. Elicit opposite decisions and explore the reasons why they were made. Consider the contingencies developed by the students.

Lead the group to a consensus about the decision to buy or wait for the next contractor to provide the materials, supplies, and equipment. Ask the class to consider the relative merits of:

- Ordering part of the equipment, such as some of the long lead-time items.

- The impact of ordering versus not ordering on the PERT and Gantt charts.

- Comparative costs of the alternative decisions, in time and money.

Summarize the value, advantages and limitations, and use of PERT and Gantt planning tools. Answer any questions about the materials covered.

Background

The mysteries of electronics as it evolved during the 1960s and 1970s led many trainers to decide that anyone planning to work in the field needed excellent grounding in mathematics as a prerequisite to the study of electronic theory.

There is little question that an electronics designer needs a thorough understanding of electronics theory and higher mathematics, but how much does an electronics equipment user or repair person require? That serious question has been asked by an increasing number of large organizations that have traditionally spent hundreds of millions of dollars training technicians in electronics theory—theory that was never applied on the job. Organizations such as the Bell Telephone System and the United States Navy realized enormous savings by eliminating parts of the training programs that did not contribute to performance on the job.

As the electronics industry moved into the 1980s, the technology became so advanced and complex that it soon became impossible to train users and repairers in all the applicable theory. Again, costs proved to be a critical factor. It became cheaper to incorporate self-diagnostic features into the equipment than to train the people to troubleshoot all the possible faults. Ironically, the more complicated electronic equipment became, the easier it was to troubleshoot and to repair.

The electronics troubleshooter and repairer must have a single prerequisite ability—the ability to read and to follow directions. The electronics hardware of today, with its associated service documentation is, in many ways, self maintaining. Repairs consist largely of replacing component parts and of performing well defined adjustments with the help of special tools.

The less sophisticated equipment requires attention, and that equipment will continue to require costly training and repair procedures. The ever-increasing maintenance costs of the older, less sophisticated equipment will hasten the demise of that hardware. In many instances, it has already become more economical to replace the outdated equipment with newer models that cost less to operate and maintain.

When preparing to develop training materials in electronics, ask questions that may not have been asked before, such as, "Do we really need to teach all that theory?" The answer may, in fact, be affirmative, but in many instances, the true answer will be negative. These answers can be supported by invoking performance objectives. The burden of proof falls on the people insisting that a particular theoretical segment is required. All you need to ask is whether or not that theory contributes to *job performance*. If it cannot be demonstrated that the theory contributes to performance, why include it in the training?

The Training Model

103
**Administration
Guide for Self-
Instructional
Training**

Troubleshooting and repairing of electronics equipment is most often best accomplished by "hands-on" exposure, demonstration, and practice. Hands-on means simply that the trainee actually handles the equipment and performs troubleshooting and repair procedures.

Typically, the following components of a training program in electronics troubleshooting and repair include:

- The actual equipment, a prototype, or a model.

- A service manual or set of instructions.

- A training manual.

- A tool kit.

- An instructor who tests the trainees' learning by measuring performance.

This kind of training can be accomplished in a laboratory setting, in a class, or on the job, where the instructor may be an experienced person who is following the prescribed training procedures. The training can even be accomplished by correspondence, perhaps with telephone support from an instructor.

The model should include one more point: the training developer should not prepare this kind of training without a qualified subject matter expert. If possible, the training developer should be trained in the job before beginning to develop the program.

Electronic equipment, more than most other kinds, changes frequently. The training should be maintained so that it reflects the actual conditions of the equipment.

Following is a sample from an electronics training program.

SAMPLE FROM AN ELECTRONICS TRAINING PROGRAM

This sample is adapted from a five-day training program developed for troubleshooting and repair of a modern electronics facsimile device. The program was developed for a large United States corporation and has been in use since the late 1970s. The program was designed to be used in a laboratory-type classroom, with an expert instructor. This presentation exemplifies only one method.

MODULE 1—INTRODUCTION

Overview

The Introduction Module will help you to become familiar with the type of training program you're starting, the format of the modules, and the course rules.

Introduction

This is a student-paced program. Every student completing this course will have achieved or exceeded a prescribed level of performance—in other words, you will have met the criteria.

Let's take a look at how you'll progress in this program. The program is divided into modules, which are convenient segments that deal either with a manageable function of the machine or with a workable section of the total training program. Each module includes an estimated time required to complete it. Use that estimate as a guide. Every module includes a Module Overview to give you an idea of what you'll be doing in the module.

Each module includes a statement of the objective for that module. The objective tells you exactly what you must do, what resources to use, and how you'll be measured to demonstrate your competence. *Since you'll be tested on the objective, it's important for you to be aware of the objective as you perform the module.* The criterion test of a module will measure your ability to meet the module objective.

The remainder of Module 1 continues in the same vein, defining the course rules and methods to be applied. It tells the student what to expect and how to proceed.

Module 2 instructs the trainees in the operation of the equipment. The module introduction includes an overview, a statement of prerequisites, the module objectives, estimated time to complete, and required resources.

Module 3 describes the machine components and their functions, following the same pattern as in Module 2.

Module 4 instructs the trainee in the use of the technical documentation describing repair of the equipment.

The remaining modules flow in logical progression, gradually building to the point where the trainee is ready for the Power Distribution Module. The material that follows is an excerpt from a self-paced program for electronics troubleshooting and repair.

Overview

In this module, you'll be locating the components of the power distribution system in the device. You'll trace the distribution of power in both the machine and in the schematics. You'll troubleshoot power distribution problems.

Prerequisite Module

Knowledge of use of technical documentation is a prerequisite.

Module Objectives

1. At the conclusion of this module, you'll demonstrate the ability to use the schematics to trace all power distribution paths in the machine.

2. You'll demonstrate the ability to locate the power distribution components in the machine.

3. You'll demonstrate the ability to troubleshoot power distribution failures, using the technical documentation.

Accuracy required is 100 percent.

Estimated Time to Complete

Two hours is the estimated time to complete.

Now, locate switch S2 (at coordinates G5) on your schematic. Switch S2 receives 5VDC from PC2 and feeds it to switch S3 (follow Flag G).

The +14VDC signal now goes to the PC5 card, where it's regulated to a constant +6.4VDC. This is the standby voltage that allows the machine's SEND and RECEIVE functions to operate. Set your meter to the +50 volt DC scale, place your red meter lead on Test Point 12 and your black lead on a good ground. Select RECEIVE MODE, place the carriage at the extreme right, and actuate the Power On switch. What does your meter read? _____VDC. What audible indication do you get? _____ This indicates the machine is ready.

Using the same setup, open the Document Door. What does your meter read now? _____VDC. What audible indication do you get? _____

The module continues with the demonstration and practice, as above, and ends with a module criterion test, consisting of troubleshooting faults inserted in the machine.

Finally, this training incorporates the use of the training manual, the technical documentation, schematics, the operator's manual, and the equipment itself. This type of training, and many others, can be made both more interesting to the trainees and more effective by using such a multimedia approach.

For many people, the term multimedia conjures up images of razzle-dazzle audio and video extravaganzas that capture the senses and grip the learner until the session is over. Multimedia may be that dramatic but, most often, multimedia training presentations reflect careful professional consideration of the most appropriate medium for the training segment presented.

When considering multimedia training, you want to select the best media to get the job done. Avoid selecting any media simply because they may be available or in vogue at the moment. Training effectiveness has been hampered in the past by applying the medium in fashion rather than the most appropriate one. Special care must be taken to avoid the rapture of new technologies, such as computers and videodisks. Learning to use the media and learning how they may effect learning should precede any commitment to such equipment. A good case in point is the wide acceptance of videotape when it became generally available in the marketplace. Many training departments purchased the expensive video equipment, having no clear idea about how to use it or whether its application would satisfy their training needs. Many of those video installations have "withered on the vine."

Don't avoid new technology, but examine it in detail, especially its potential application to your training programs.

Not all multimedia training is elaborate or inappropriate, by any means. Much professionally developed self-administered training used today may be classified as multimedia, especially those programs that require more than a simple reading exercise. Skills training is particularly adapted to a multimedia approach. For example, a training program designed to teach electronics may use a combination of written materials, audio tapes, an electronic multimeter, and a kit of electronic parts. Each of those devices represents a different medium—thus, we have a multimedia self-administered training program. It's actually more difficult to design single than multimedia training because a single medium limits the designer in presentation of the materials.

One of the major problems with self-administered training programs is that of maintaining learner interest at a level sufficiently high to ensure completion of the training.

Multimedia presentations are usually more interesting to the learners than the one-dimensional programs, thereby increasing or at least maintaining the motivational levels of the trainees. The more interesting a training program is to the learners, the more likely that it will be pursued by them.

Variety is the spice of training, as well as of life. When designing training materials, consider the degree of learner concentration required to complete the segment. Consider the degree of motivation required to stay with the materials to completion. Consider the general level of interest inherent in the material.

It is an established practice to break the routine after about one hour of intensive work in the classroom. You can build in breaks in your training materials by suggesting that the learner take a ten-minute break, but the learners in self-administered programs will take breaks whenever they desire. An effective "break" can be a switch to another medium, as shown in the example. Note the transitions from the printed medium to the machine, and to a different written medium. Using more than one instance of the same medium introduces variety also. A workbook and a reference manual are both print media, but they may be different enough in their appearance and use to be considered as variations of the print medium. They serve to maintain a level of learner interest when applied judiciously.

On the following pages you will find a sample of a self-administered training program.

This example is an excerpt from a self-administered training program designed to teach professionals the use of a computer-based management information system. The workers have computer terminals at their desks or nearby. The learners are at their terminals and have a user's manual and a workbook. They have already spent about thirty minutes in the program.

The Terminal

You can retrieve data from a variety of terminals. Some of the terminals provide you with printed information, while others display the data on cathode ray tubes (CRT).

Basically, the operating principles are the same, regardless of the terminal type. Find Appendix A in your user's manual. Read page A-1 and look at pages A-2 and A-3. They should be similar to the terminal you have in front of you.

If your terminal is like the one shown, the OFF/ON switch is located at the right rear corner. Be sure the terminal is plugged in, and then turn the terminal on. There's a slight hum when it's on.

On page A-21 is a description of the keys and their functions. Be sure there is paper in the terminal if it's the printer type. Type your name, just to get the feel for the keyboard and how it reacts to your touch. You aren't connected to the computer yet, so none of your actions has any impact on the system. Ignore the BREAK key for the moment and use the other keys as described on page A-4. Continue to use the keyboard until you feel comfortable with it.

Logging On

Next, we'll connect to the computer, after you record some important information. Open your Retrieval Aid to the first window, LOGGING ON. Remove the card from the holder and write down all the information indicated by the blank spaces. Memorize your password. Do not write it on the card. Replace the card in the holder. Now, dial the telephone number you recorded in the Aid. If the line is busy, try the alternate number or wait a few minutes and try again.

The phone will ring normally a number of times and will be answered with a high-pitched tone. That tone is your signal that the computer is ready to connect to your terminal. Insert the telephone receiver into the coupler—those two rubber cups at the rear of the terminal. Be sure that the telephone wire is at the end indicated on the terminal. Push the receiver all the way into the cups.

There is a Carrier Detector Light (usually a green lamp at the lower right side of the keyboard) that will come on when the connection between the computer and the terminal is completed. If the green light doesn't come on within a few seconds, you must hang up the telephone and begin the procedure again. Be sure the ON LINE switch (in the lower right corner, near the light) is in the ON LINE position.

Press the RETURN key twice.

Now turn in the user's manual to page V-2.

Begin at Step 6. The remainder of the process is straightforward. You can use the information you recorded on the Aid card in response to the computer's request for that information. Do not type the quotation marks, as they appear in the manual. The notation (CR) means that you should press the RETURN key (the RETURN key is usually a different color from the other keys).

Perform all the steps through Step 16.

If the response is not immediate, that's because other people are using the computer. Response time varies; sometimes it will be very fast, while at other times it will be quite slow. As long as the Carrier Detector Light is on, you're connected to the computer. When response time is slow, you may use the time to review the retrieval strategy you plan to use.

When the system asks you to enter the name of the module you're going to use, type the name and then press the RETURN key, as described in the middle of page V-3 of your user's manual.

Continue reading on that page and follow the directions until you're asked to type 1 or 2. Type: 2(CR). You will then see the message, ENTER COMMAND.

The system is requesting that you tell it what to do. It will wait for you to enter a command.

16

Lesson Plans

A lesson plan is like a roadmap, a scenario, or a schedule of activities—it guides the instructor step-by-step through the instructional program. The instructor's lesson plan is the organization of the lesson materials, prepared to help to deliver the training.

Lesson plans take many forms and contain varying levels of detail, but every instructor uses some form of lesson plan, even if nothing is written on paper. An instructor may form mental images of the presentation, thinking, "I'll start with topic A and, if there aren't any problems with it, I'll move into topic D. If the students have trouble with the topic A concepts, I'll go to topic B." That is a lesson plan.

A lesson plan may take the form of a detailed list of activities for the instructor to perform through each phase of the training. It may take the form of an outline; it may be an annotated outline or text, with highlighted sections; it may be notes in the margins of the student textbook; it may be combinations; or it may even take other forms.

The lesson plan may be prepared by someone else for the instructor, but the lesson plan used in the classroom is ultimately one that is prepared by the instructor. Even if the lesson plan is prepared as a script, asking the instructor to use the words as presented, the instructor is sure to change something, even if it is only in the reading of the lines.

If you're developing training materials to be presented by other people, consideration of the lesson plan format may be critical to the success or failure of the program. For example, if you know the instructors who will be presenting the materials and you know that they use a certain kind of lesson plan successfully, it could be courting disaster to present them with a different kind of lesson plan to use in this program. If possible, solicit input from the instructors to establish the kind of lesson plan you'll prepare and how it will be used. If you can accomplish that, the probability of your developing a successful program is increased.

If it's impossible to determine who the instructors will be or what their lesson plan preferences are, design a lesson plan that offers maximum flexibility and adaptability, including suggestions for adapting the materials to the instructor's own formats. The final format could be an outline of points to be covered, or it might be any of the other kinds of lesson plan formats.

The essential points to remember about lesson plans are:

- There is *always* a lesson plan in the classroom, even if it's only a mental one.

- The lesson plan determines, to a considerable degree, how the materials will be presented and how they will be received by the trainees.

- The lesson plan you prepare will be modified to some degree by the instructors, even if you are ultimately the instructor.

- The training developer should offer the instructor guidance for modification of the prepared lesson plan.

**USE OF LESSON
PLANS**

Some instructors use every conceivable device in the classroom. Their primary concern is to get the material across to the trainees. They will use materials provided to them in ways that are not suggested by the author and will invent classroom techniques to suit their needs.

Some instructors will use the lesson plans provided as a guide, staying reasonably close to the materials, but adjusting and adapting, as necessary.

Still other instructors will follow the lesson plan slavishly, without varying from the materials for any reason. If the lesson plan is written as a script, these instructors will read or memorize the materials and present them as prescribed.

The difference in the instructors' use of the lesson plans is determined largely by their experience and knowledge of the subject. An experienced instructor who is very familiar with the subject will generally use the lesson plans the least, while the inexperienced instructor who has minimal knowledge of the subject will probably be the one to follow the lesson plans most closely.

Among the more difficult tasks in developing training is estimating how much time is required to complete the program. While a number of guides can help make the time estimates more accurate, the best method for establishing time requirements is empirical—a vital part of the training development is a collection of timing data.

Some training program elements are easier than others to estimate accurately. For example, if you're asking the trainees to perform a specific task or a test, you can set a time limit and hold to it. You can also limit your review of a test or a session to a specific amount of time.

The difficult activities to time are those that are open ended—where the lesson plan states, "Lead a discussion of the point until you're satisfied that the trainees understand it." Such discussions may require five minutes or an hour, unless the points under discussion are subdivided such that the minimum and maximum times are close to being identical.

Breaking the material into small, manageable segments makes it easier to estimate the times accurately, but when the materials call for the trainees to practice a skill, such as soldering a connection, some trainees will perform perfectly the first time, while others may require several trials, each of which takes time. It's virtually impossible to estimate accurately in those cases. Even after testing the program, it's possible that some of the activities will vary so much from class to class that they will remain untimed.

Timing is important when there isn't enough time allocated to complete the essential parts of the program. If some objectives cannot be met because insufficient time is scheduled, some redesign is required to either change some of the objectives or to build a different strategy for their achievement. It may be possible to develop alternative strategies for the program where time has been impossible to estimate. In such cases, certain aspects of the program should be included only if sufficient time remains after completion of the essential elements. Such decisions should be made in conjunction with the program sponsor, the training developers, and the instructors.

Samples of several lesson plans follow.

Similarities and Differences

It's essential that you emphasize the point that many of the nonverbal communication devices *are not universal.*

Encourage the participants to take some time after arriving in a new country to observe and ask questions about the meanings of various gestures and other nonverbal communications. They should pay particular attention to those nonverbal communications that are taboo.

Foreign nationals expect newly arrived Americans to be relatively ignorant of their customs and language. This may be considered to be a reprieve by the new Administrative Officer, but it's only temporary. Even the Administrative Officers are expected by the foreign nationals to be interested enough in the culture of the country to learn at least some of the nonverbal communications used by the people. Failure to do so could make the tour a very long and painful one for the Administrative Officer.

The same holds true for verbal communications, but generally to a lesser extent. It's important to know that there are words in English that mean different things in other languages and can cause severe embarrassment, to say the least. It's particularly important to become familiar with the local slang, since some words or expressions that may be formulated from a dictionary could be offensive to the local population.

Using the activities list you've put on the chalkboard, explain the use, value, and limitations of Gantt charting and PERT diagramming. Include the following points in your discussion:

- Preparing any type of chart forces the user to think about the entire program and the relationships among the activities.

- The charts are a form of communication, informing others of precisely what is expected, and when.

- The charts give the manager a picture of the expected status at any point in the program.

- Maintenance of the charts can be time consuming, but each time a chart is updated, the manager's knowledge of the program status is updated.

- Performers and managers have the same understanding of the activities to be performed and when they are due for completion.

Describe how a Gantt chart is prepared.
Explain that this type of chart is also called a timeline or waterfall chart. The essential elements of this type of chart are:

- Activity title or description.

- Activities which typically require a period of time for completion; for example, "Appoint a manager" would not usually be found on a Gantt chart.

- Calendar time from start to finish of each activity.

- Level of labor resource to be applied is sometimes included.

- Cost information is rarely included.

117

This segment is oriented toward Objective 3, giving the trainees the ability to counsel employees in overseas locations.

Put into your own words the concepts that follow and write major points on the chalkboard as you proceed.

Counseling overseas employees effectively requires an understanding of the subtleties of the culture and nonverbal communication devices used locally. Fortunately for the new supervisor, the successful overseas employees make adjustments for the new staff arriving at the overseas location. As indicated earlier, there is a grace period, during which the new supervisor is given time to get on board. The grace period should be used for observing and asking questions of the experienced staff personnel.

Point out that it's important to know which of the experienced personnel to ask. Unfortunately, there are still some old line supervisors who may be at that location for years, making little or no effort to learn how to communicate effectively with the overseas employees. Those people should not be consulted on this subject.

The new supervisor will soon learn which of the overseas employees are willing to be supportive; they can be invaluable to the newcomer.

If the new supervisor behaves as though there is nothing to be learned, the tour will likely be very long.

The overseas employees have a significant impact on the quality of everyday life at the work location. The attitudes of the new supervisor have a substantial influence on the overall quality of life at the overseas location.

People in different cultures respond differently to authority, as represented by the supervisor. Some people expect the supervisor to take charge and to be authoritarian, while others expect a less paternalistic and more democratic approach. Counseling cannot be effective until the supervisor determines the style in that locale.

Perhaps one of the most effective ways to establish interpersonal relationships in any culture is to show a *sincere* interest in people as individuals without patronizing them. The kinds of things to be interested in include their country, its language, culture, geography, customs, and other "neutral" aspects of life in the country. Personal interests should be avoided in virtually all instances. If overseas employees volunteer personal information, it should be listened to with the same kind of interest, but further probing or other personal questions should be avoided by the supervisor. A key point: *People like to talk about themselves* and to be helpful if the situation is free of *perceived* threat to them. Discuss these kinds of things with the overseas employees at off-duty times. Interfering with the ongoing local activities could be disruptive and, therefore, be perceived as threatening. The conversations should be natural, as opposed to appearing contrived.

Paraphrasing is a useful device, especially when in a new or strange environment. Paraphrasing is stating the other person's ideas in your own words, or giving an example that shows you think you know what the other person is

118

talking about. A good paraphrase is usually more specific than the original statement was. Before agreeing or disagreeing with a remark, it's useful to express your understanding, thus enabling the other person to clarify any misunderstandings.

Checking your perception of what the other person is feeling conveys the message, "I want to understand your feelings. Is this really the way you feel about it?"

When checking your perception, you are identifying the other person's feelings, as, for example, "disappointed," "frustrated," "pleased," etc. You are *not* expressing approval or disapproval of those feelings. You're conveying, "This is how I perceive you are feeling. Am I accurate?"

Your perception of the feelings often results more from what *you* are feeling, than from the other person's words, tone, gestures, facial expressions, etc. Our inferences about other people's feelings can be, and often are, inaccurate, so it's important to check them out. Try to convey that you want to understand the other as a person—and that means understanding that person's feelings. It also helps you to avoid statements or actions that are inappropriate because they are based on false assumptions about what the other person is feeling.

Describing behavior of the other person tells what you observed—behavior that anyone could see.

The trainees should be cautioned to avoid assigning unfavorable motives, intentions, or character traits to others. Supervisors should restrict their behavior to respond exclusively to what is observed.

Suggest to the class that they can improve their skill in describing behavior by careful observation of other people's behavior. As they do, they may find that some of their conclusions were based less on observable evidence than on their own feelings. Accusations are usually expressions of feelings.

Questioning is a useful device and is used in three ways:

1. To elicit information.

2. To put forth an idea or a suggestion.

3. To reject an idea or a suggestion.

Listening to almost any conversation will show that questioning to elicit information is used least. Most questions either will be disguised ideas and suggestions or disguised rejections of those ideas and suggestions.

To develop skill in framing questions, the trainee needs to learn to probe for suggestions and ideas in the questions of others and to paraphrase when they think a person has used a question to reject an idea or a suggestion. This process may help the trainee to heighten awareness of how the trainee is using questioning.

Asking open-ended questions whenever possible is also useful. Encourage the trainees to say, "How useful was . . . ?" rather than "Was that useful?" The open-ended questions elicit more information from the other person.

Active listening, other than note-taking, means checking for understanding frequently rather than waiting for long or complicated inputs to end. When it's used appropriately, it is not usually considered to be interruption.

Active listening also means attending to the nonverbal communications. Being aware of gestures, posture, facial expressions, and tone of voice helps the trainee to become a more effective active listener.

Active listening also involves your nonverbal response to what the other person is saying. Nodding the head, smiling, posture, etc. are all parts of active listening. The difference between active and passive listening is the difference between including yourself in the total message from the other person, and not involving yourself.

17

Examples of Other Types of Training Materials

Case studies are a proven technique to involve the participants personally in problem or conflict situations. Ideally, the reader will identify with one of the principals in the case or will remain at the other extreme, able to bring complete objectivity to the situation. The case study should always be tied to a training objective. In other words, try to accomplish some specific learning with the case.

You may want the learner to use the case materials to prepare for an encounter, or you may simply want to expose the learner to different viewpoints surrounding an issue. Whatever your objective, several points should be kept in mind when preparing and using case materials.

In general, a case study contains three parts:

1. Background, or introduction, that sets up the situation and develops relationships among the principals and the events leading to the situation.

2. Conflict, or problem situation, in which sufficient detail is presented so the reader can comprehend all the relevant facts. Alternatives may be presented for reader considera-

tion, and to build strong arguments for all sides of the problem and the solutions.

3. Resolution, or conclusion, in which the situation is brought to a point where all arguments have been completed and the principals must act. The consequences of the actions are considered and the actions are defined. Questions may be included to guide the reader through the material to a conclusion.

There may or may not be a "school solution" to the case, depending on your objectives and other factors, such as whether the case was taken from real life, and where the actions and their results are documented. Usually, you'll want to include in the instructor's materials either a "school solution," the results of a real case, or guidelines to lead the participants to a workable conclusion.

The example that follows is a fictitious case that could be adapted to virtually any conflict situation in any organization. You could convert the conflict development to suit the needs of your training objectives and program.

Background

You're the financial manager in an office machine leasing operation and you've known Pat, the sales manager, for more than five years. Pat had been the sales manager in this office for twenty-two months. Pat compiled a superior record of increased sales and customer satisfaction in the area office before coming to this one. Pat has always been proud of getting along with everyone.

Pat, as a member of the sales force, considers his job successful when the products are not only placed, but stay in the customers' hands.

You've always gotten along well with Pat and you've had no problems working together in the past. You know that Pat's every waking breath is spent selling, keeping customers happy, and pressing the sales force to outdo its previous superior performance. It's a hard-driving operation, and a successful one, by any standard. Pat knows you've got a job to do also. Over the past year, in particular, you've had considerable impact on Pat's thinking because you've taken the trouble to explain your job and your responsibilities in terms that are meaningful to sales people. During this period, you've gone so far as to accompany Pat on customer calls. You've walked in each other's shoes, so you each have a pretty good understanding of the job the other is doing.

Accounts in Arrears

You've been struggling to bring your receivables into line, but there are still some customers who have been evasive and have not paid. You've tried everything you could think of—and most of the delinquent accounts have been resolved.

You called on Pat to assist, and the cooperation couldn't have been better. Your working relationship with Pat during the past few months has been unusually good.

However, three accounts are more than 180 days in arrears, and you feel compelled to take whatever action is required to clear the books. Something must be done soon or Headquarters will be all over you for failure to resolve the outstanding accounts.

At the same time, you know that the only way to clear the accounts may be to reclaim some equipment. Reclaiming equipment, you're certain, will not make Pat happy, to put it mildly. Each piece of equipment that's reclaimed is deducted from the sales performance figures. It seems a shame to risk alienating the sales manager, especially since you've had such an outstanding working relationship.

Your credit manager shares your concern and has thought long and hard about how to solve the problem without incurring the wrath of the entire sales department. You've called the customers and you've written to them, but still no satisfactory resolution has been found.

The Acme Jargon Company has had two of your smaller machines for the past two years. The account was current until about eight months ago, when they started slipping a little at a time. No payment has been made in over four months. When you phoned, they said that their business had dropped off substantially, but they felt the condition was temporary and they requested more time. In fact, they have written several times, requesting extensions. You believe there is a reasonable expectation that the amounts due will be paid and you're willing to go along with their requests, especially since the total balance remains relatively low. You've talked to Pat about the account and the two of you have concluded that the customer is basically a good risk and will eventually settle the account satisfactorily.

The Keystone Arch Company presents a somewhat different picture. They have actually added two pieces of moderately priced equipment to their existing higher priced machine—and they have been ordering supplies in large quantities. This is a red flag account, more than 180 days in arrears, with an increasingly large outstanding balance. Immediate attention is required. Your credit manager has written and phoned, but has been unable to get any payment or promise of any. You've visited Keystone to discuss the status of the account and found them to be pleasant, but noncommittal when asked about a payment schedule. Their attitude seemed to be that if we didn't like the situation, we could take the machines. They know where they could get replacements immediately—from the competition.

The third customer, Stone Corner Structures, is a large account with a wide variety of your equipment. They have a rather large monthly bill for machines and for supplies. The Stone company has been a customer for twelve years, and the records show that they have never been among the fast payers. They've managed to maintain the account always 30–60 days in arrears. They've always paid within 180 days, but no payment has been made for the past six months. Your credit manager's calls and collection letters have not even produced a response from Stone.

The credit manager has proposed a plan to resolve these accounts. The strategy requires cooperation from the sales department. You've tried to plan so that neither the customers, your company, nor the sales force is affected negatively. You want to go over your strategy with Pat because part of your plan may result in reclaiming some machines.

The Strategy

Here's what you present to Pat.

For the Acme Jargon Company, you plan to propose a partial payment plan if they agree to pay 30 percent of the total amount due within ten days and then maintain a monthly payment schedule equal to 25 percent of the outstanding balance, while paying current bills. You believe there is a good chance that Acme will accept the terms, and the real payoff is that you'll retain a valued customer who may become even a larger user in the future. You're prepared to shave the requirements by 5 percent on both the initial payment and on the monthly payments. If Acme won't agree to an acceptable payment schedule, you're going to have to reclaim the equipment. There is no way you can leave machines at an account that is so far in arrears, unless there is a satisfactory payment schedule.

The Keystone Arch account is a more serious matter because there is considerably more at stake than at Acme. The three machines at Keystone consume large quantities of supplies and generate substantial use charges. Consequently, your plan is somewhat more complex. You plan to propose to Keystone that they pay 25 percent of the outstanding balance within ten days, and that the account be brought current within sixty days, with half the balance to be paid each month. Your fallback position is to grant a low interest note, payable each month until the account is current. If the customer doesn't agree to your proposal, you will support the credit manager by reclaiming the machines and will turn the account over for collection or legal action.

The Stone account, you've decided, needs to be given a boost so their payments become more regular and substantial. As financial manager, you plan to visit Stone so you can point out to them that they really are in a position to cause damage to their fine credit rating. You'd like to set an example for your Credit section by returning with a signed check that would bring the account to at least the ninety-day level. You're prepared to press reasonably hard for payment. Reclaiming the equipment from this account is something you don't even want to think about because the repercussions would be felt half-way around the world. Any decision to reclaim the equipment from this account, you feel, would have to be shared by your superiors at Headquarters.

With your strategies in mind, you call Pat and set up a meeting to discuss the three problem accounts. You tell Pat that the reason for the meeting is to jointly address several serious problem accounts. In fact, you had asked Pat previously to check with the sales staff for the credit pull list for the three accounts to determine if there is some information that could influence your decisions. Pat is agreeable, but is so busy that the meeting can't be scheduled until the 15th, and today is only the 2nd of the month. You agree and tell Pat that you'll do some more work on the accounts in the meantime. You plan to make some more phone calls and visit the accounts, if necessary.

The meeting date arrives, and you've had no luck in the interim. The accounts are virtually the same as they were in the beginning, except now they are two weeks' further in arrears. You go to the conference room you had scheduled for the meeting with Pat. Pat arrives about five minutes late, but is apologetic and as personable as ever. You get down to business right away. There isn't much time for small talk. Besides, you want to impress Pat with the seriousness of the situation. You describe the three cases to Pat, explaining why accounts aged more than sixty days are unacceptable and that they represent a generally poor business practice. After you describe the three accounts, the conversation goes as follows:

Pat: "It sure looks like we've got to do something—but what if they don't pay, no matter what we do?"

You: "I've tried everything I could think of. Did you come up with anything that might be useful?"

Pat: "I explained the situation to the sales reps and asked if they knew of any reason for the state of those accounts. The only thing they were able to come up with was that Stone Structures was rumored to be in financial trouble and may be on the verge of bankruptcy. The sales rep didn't really think that was true because they're thinking of upgrading their present equipment. In fact, the sales rep expects to close the deal in the next week or two."

You: "Anything on the others?"

Pat: "No."

You: "I've thought long and hard about these accounts and came up with a set of plans I'd like to go over with you."

Pat: "Good."
(You explain the details of the strategy and plan for each account to Pat.)

Pat: "WOW! I don't know if we can do what you're trying to accomplish. If it comes to reclaiming any machines, you're going to risk losing some friends. You know the biggest contest in years is on now and, if we lose even one small piece, we run the risk of losing that Hawaii trip, among other things. Besides, we've been getting enough cancellations without doing suicidal things like pulling them out of old-time accounts. They'll pay eventually."

You: "I hope you're right, but we just can't wait. Headquarters will be all over me if I let these accounts go any longer."

Pat: "You know that this is the first time ever that our outfit is in the running to be tops in the region, and we don't want to blow it. The boss wouldn't appreciate your pulling any equipment right now, either. Lou is trying very hard to ensure that we come out number one this year. Lou's pretty ambitious and has one eye on a promotion to Headquarters."

You: "I know, but what else can we do if they don't pay?"

Pat: "I don't know, but you'd better not reclaim any equipment."

You: "How about calling on the accounts with me to see if we can't do something together to get them to pay?"

Pat: "Gee, I'd really like to, but we're right in the middle of this big campaign. I just don't have the time right now. Besides, you don't really think it'll do any good, do you?"

You: "I'm the perennial optimist, but I don't know if we'll get anything or not. To be perfectly frank, chances appear to be pretty slim, but I've got to do something right away."

Pat: "Do something—just so whatever you do, you don't reclaim even one piece. Consider that a friendly warning."

You: "I may have to. . . ."

Pat: "Don't even think that way. We can't afford to lose a single piece, and

I'll be forced to go to Lou to stop you from reclaiming any machines.''

You: "That isn't very friendly."

Pat: "What can I say? You've got your job to do, and I've got mine."

Conclusion

The meeting started out as a cooperative venture, with both parties discussing "their" problem. It deteriorated into statements of self-interest, threats, finally a break, and possibly a damaged friendship.

Go back to the case and think about the questions that follow. You may want to make some notes to aid your discussion when you come to class to discuss this case.

Questions

1. How might you have planned to deal with this case differently?

2. What might you have done to avoid reaching such a point with Pat?

3. How might you have gotten Pat to participate further in the solution to the problems?

4. What options are open to you now?

5. Should you reclaim any machines, in accordance with your plan?

6. What will Pat do if you reclaim any machines?

7. How might you repair the damage done to your relationship with Pat?

8. What resources do you have to combat any barriers Pat may erect if you decide to reclaim any machines?

9. What is or should be the role of headquarters in this matter?

10. What are the best things that could happen in this situation?

11. What are the worst things that could happen in this situation?

12. What might you have done wrong?

13. What did Pat do wrong?

14. What did you do right?

15. What did Pat do right?

AUTO-ADAPTIVE TRAINING

Auto-adaptive training uses methods different from the traditional ones. You should be aware of a number of major differences.

Perhaps the major difference between this program and other training is that the manager (or a designee) is responsible to guide and assist the trainee through the training. There is no instructor in the usual sense. There are no classroom sessions, no homework, and no examinations; training is an integral part of the daily job.

An example of auto-adaptive training follows.

Most training programs have an established time period for completion. This program has been designed for you to use either before you begin your job in procurement or after you've begun to perform procurement functions. The time required to complete this program will vary according to your needs and the needs of your organization. If you're just beginning your career in procurement, it's quite probable that you'll require a year or more to complete the modules contained in this notebook.

The learning is based on your needs and the needs of your organization. You and your manager will arrange the program to meet all those needs, at a pace that's comfortable and meaningful to you and to your organization.

The learning includes experiences of performing the procurement functions through simulations and real procurement requests. Your manager and you will discuss the reasons for the different activities, the decisions required for their completion, and their results.

One result of the training is that you'll be developing action plans for the improvement of the procurement function in your organization.

As you complete each part of the training, the notebook becomes a reference manual that you should use continually. Each time you learn a new procedure or fact, you make notes in your manual, thereby making it increasingly valuable as a reference. You are building your own, personalized reference materials to aid you in your daily work in procurement. The manual should prove invaluable if you're ever asked to support the training of others in the future. You should set aside whatever time is necessary to maintain the notebook.

This introductory program covers the basic functions and activities required by all procurement people. The materials are entirely consistent with established policies and are tailored to your organization's standard procedures. The designers of this program recognize that there are differences among the different organizations and locations throughout the world. These materials allow for the necessary modification to suit those different needs, within the framework of the basic policies and regulations.

The modules are presented in a specific order that should be followed. While you may find it desirable to follow a different path, you're advised to begin with Module 1 and proceed through all modules in sequence. However, if you're experienced in procurement and want only to confirm your understanding or review some of the materials, you should feel free to use the materials in the manner most useful to you.

The modules have been prepared in a sequence most appropriate to a new procurement person. They begin with a general introduction to the procurement process and proceed through contract negotiation, as follows:

Module 1—Introduction. The introduction is heavily oriented toward providing you with experiences that help you understand your own organization better, its methods of doing business, and the policies and procedures that govern its procurement activities. You'll begin the development of action plans that you'll update throughout the remaining modules.

Module 2—Ethics. The ethics of buying have been well documented and are considered by your management as perhaps the most important aspect of the professional buyers' approach to the procurement process. The module includes several activities and discussions with your own management and other professional procurement people.

Module 3—The Procurement Process. This module serves to introduce the remaining four modules by defining the procurement process elements as Source Selection, Quotation, Cost Analysis, and Negotiation. Modules 3–7 should generally be done in sequence, since each module leads logically into the next.

Module 4—Source Selection. This module presents methods and criteria for identification of suitable suppliers for materials and services and includes practice in the identification of sources and in preparation of requests for quotation (RFQ). There is emphasis on the need for precision when sending RFQs to suppliers.

Module 5—Quotation. This module leads you into the techniques for assessing the responsiveness of vendor quotations and the beginning of the cost analysis process.

Module 6—Cost Analysis. You learn to perform the kinds of analyses that help determine which vendors to select for final negotiation.

Module 7—Negotiation. In this final module, you'll negotiate the terms, conditions, and price for the products or services you need. You'll update your action plan to include all the learning to this point. You'll have several consultations with your manager and with other experts in your organization.

A Module Assessment Report can be found at the end of each module. You should complete the forms as accurately and promptly as possible and submit them as indicated on the forms. If you have questions or requests that cannot be handled in your own organization, please contact the senior procurement manager at Headquarters. If you need further information about the procurement process, we'd appreciate receiving it from you.

We wish you well in your learning and in your career as a professional procurement person.

(Following is a sample module, covering cost analysis.)

Summary Activities

This summary activities list provides an overview of the module contents and also permits an alternative learning method where less reading is required than in the longer version.

The subject and content of both methods are identical, but this summary form is intended for use by people whose first language is not English, and for those who may already be experienced with the subject.

Procedure

Meet with your manager, who will explain how to go about the training activities of this module. You will perform a series of activities, as outlined in the next section. You will meet with your manager at several points during the module execution. Your manager will inform you when you have successfully met the requirements of this module.

All your questions about this training should be directed to your manager or the person designated by your manager.

Activities

1. Read the note at the beginning of the module.

2. Read the Module 6 learning objectives and discuss them with your manager.

3. Read the introduction to the module.

4. Review your files to perform cost analysis procedures on previous procurements.

5. Perform cost analysis procedures on the quotations from the files and from the quotations from the Appendix in Module 5. Use the Cost Estimate Form and the Cost Analysis Checklist.

6. Prepare an action plan to improve cost analysis procedures in your organization. Meet with other experts in your organization for assistance. Discuss your conclusions and your plan with your manager.

7. Perform the exercise, as defined in the module.

8. Ask for any expert help you may need. Discuss the module contents with your manager.

MODULE ASSESSMENT REPORT

MODULE NUMBER _____ DATE _____/_____/_____ NAME _____

LOCATION _____ ORGANIZATION _____

PLEASE RATE THE FOLLOWING ON A SCALE OF 1–5 (5 IS BEST):

1. OVERALL ASSESSMENT OF THE MODULE _____

2. RELEVANCE OF THE MODULE TO THE JOB _____

3. CLARITY OF THE MATERIALS _____

4. INTEREST LEVEL OF THE MATERIALS _____

5. DIFFICULTY OF THE MATERIALS _____

6. ACCURACY OF THE MATERIALS _____

7. DEGREE OF CONFIDENCE IN PERFORMING THE ACTIVITIES
   LEARNED IN THIS MODULE _____

8. WHAT DID YOU LIKE BEST ABOUT THE MODULE? _____
   _____
   _____

9. WHAT DID YOU LIKE LEAST ABOUT THE MODULE? _____
   _____
   _____

10. WHAT CHANGES WOULD YOU MAKE TO THE MODULE? _____
    _____
    _____

11. PLEASE MAKE ANY OTHER COMMENTS YOU FEEL MIGHT BE USEFUL
    TO THE TRAINING PROGRAM DEVELOPERS _____
    _____
    _____
    _____
    _____

Some training materials take the form of guidelines and restated information, designed to make often uninteresting or obscure material more informative and more accessible to the people who need it to perform their jobs.

The following example of *Policies and Practices* represents a segment of that kind of presentation.

Understanding management philosophy may be the beginning of your job as a manager. But it's just the beginning.

There remains the task—and the challenge—of implementing this philosophy day by day on the job.

The issues that confront you are diverse, constant, and sometimes unique; they usually have more than one solution.

There is no pat answer to any of them. But it is expected that you'll bring to each one a thoughtful, informed, and disciplined approach.

These guidelines have been prepared to help you do just that.

Here you'll find the most critical management policies and practices you need to understand and how to apply them.

You'll find your responsibilities clearly spelled out. And you'll find the critical points that should guide you as you turn principle into practice.

These guidelines should be your daily companion for the work that is performed under your direction.

COMMUNICATIONS

Intent

Open communications among all levels of employees is essential to effective operations. The basic intent of the communications program is to provide all employees with the information they need to perform their jobs effectively and to understand the mission and direction of the organization and their own operating units.

We guarantee employees the freedom to express ideas and concerns about their jobs and work environment to management without fear of any adverse effect on job status or working relationships.

Managers' Responsibilities

You have the primary responsibility for communicating with your employees and for providing a working environment that freely invites candid two-way communication.

Your role is especially important in interpreting and sponsoring discussion about topics of concern to employees. These topics may be addressed through various media—including local publications—but it's up to you to personalize this information and relate it to the employees' work.

Critical Points

You're expected to carry out the following communication guidelines:

- Responsibility for the success of the communications program rests with all managers.

- Communications leadership in any organization is the responsibility of that organization's senior management.

- All managers are responsible to their own managers and to their people for communicating information on the state of business, the tasks and goals of the organization, and the progress of the organization's work.

- Managers owe it to their subordinates to pass employees' concerns and questions upward and to press for timely and responsive answers.

- Managers are responsible to their employees for candid communications regarding an individual's performance and career aspirations, and for resolving misunderstandings of the organization's policy and its applications.

- Employee self-esteem, as well as the quality of work life, can only be protected through continuing interpersonal and intergroup communication between employees and management.

- The senior manager in each unit has the responsibility to maintain an appropriate employee communications program for the organization.

- All managers have an obligation to their employees to be forthright and timely in discussing objectives, results, problems, difficulties, and opportunities.

These guidelines continue in the same vein, providing information to managers in a form more abbreviated than in the source materials. Care must be taken when dealing with policy to ensure proper management approval before release. Your interpretation, while probably correct, may include emphases different from those desired by senior management. It pays to obtain senior management review and approval.

Chapter 3
CAI Authoring

The most difficult part of the authoring job is designing the Lesson. You must identify the course objectives or concepts to be learned and you must develop a mini-lesson or topic for each objective. You can string several topics together in one lesson, or you can have one topic per lesson. If you follow the sample lesson format shown under Lesson Control in Chapter 2 of this user's manual, then you'll need to write an abstract or summary of the lesson material for the B student. This would be your screen format 3. Then you'll need a little more detail, your screen format 4, to provide the help required by the C student.

You have the option of including drill questions, after the review material, or you can require your students to repeat from the beginning, until they understand the material.

For the first few times you author a lesson, follow the steps exactly as they're given here. As you increase your facility with the system, you'll develop your own techniques and variations. When you do, let us know so your experiences may be shared with others.

Here are the steps for authoring (if you're already in CAIWARE-2D then skip to Step 4):

1. Turn off the expansion interface and the keyboard-CPU. Then turn on the expansion interface and the CPU. This resets all RAM memory.

2. Place the author's diskette in drive 0, and press the reset button on the left rear of your keyboard. (Your working copies of the diskettes should not have write protects, because the system writes the lesson on the author's diskette, and it writes the response file on the student's diskette. Note that the instructions here assume that you have the minimum system of 32K memory and one drive. If you have a second drive, then you can direct the system to write the Lesson file and the Response file on any drive you choose.)

3. Respond to the prompts as follows (user response is shown in upper case):

> How many files? 1   (Type 1 and press ENTER)
> Memory size?—   (If you have 48K user memory then type 48500. If 32K just press ENTER)
>
> Radio Shack Disk Basic
>   Version 2.2
> Ready
> >RUN"CAI"   (Press ENTER)

How many disk drives are connected (1 to 4)?	(Type the NUMBER)
Please enter today's date (mmddyy):	(Type the DATE)
Hour (00–23):	(Type HOUR in military time)
Minutes (00–59):	(Type MINUTES)
Seconds (00–59):	(Type SECONDS)

18

Applications of Computers in Training

Computers were being used to aid human learning long before the term "computer" was in general use. Early analog computers were used in planetaria to display the changing pictures of the skies. The early pilot training simulators made use of similar analog devices, which were gradually displaced by digital techniques.

The advent of electronic digital computers permitted a wide variety of applications to training. Sophisticated simulations in real- and non-real-time applications became feasible in the 1950s, and are found today in numerous complex military systems, including aircraft crew trainers, ships' systems, and decision-making models. The use of computers in training, while not new, is barely out of its infancy. The potential for using the computer in training on a more widespread basis has been retarded by a number of factors, not the least significant of which has been cost.

Another equally important factor that has kept computer-aided training applications at a relatively low level is that many of the early applications failed because they didn't take advantage of the inherent power of the computer—they merely used the computer to turn the pages of a book. Such use discouraged many potential users from exploring the potential value of computers in training. Two

139

other factors impeded the progress of computers in training: (1) the costs of the computers were high, and (2) the time required to prepare training materials not only required extensive learning of the computer language and systems but much time was required to prepare training materials for the computers.

Still, some progress was made in the use of computers for training in a number of businesses, universities, some school systems, and in the military. The costs remained high and the results were less than spectacular, with some notable exceptions, and work continues to this time. In fact, work in this field is growing at a faster rate than ever before, due largely to the advent of the microprocessor which introduced low-cost computing and made it generally available. The microprocessor is the basis of the personal computer that has found a huge market in homes, offices, and schools. Widespread use of computer-based training has begun to expand rapidly.

The terminology in the field of computers in training may be confusing, primarily because different names are given to the same process. To this date, there has been no standardization of the term describing the process. You'll see the following terms, all of which mean the presentation and manipulation of instructional materials, mediated by a computer:

- Computer Based Instruction (CBI).

- Computer Aided Instruction (CAI).

- Computer Assisted Training (CAT).

- Computer Aided Learning (CAL).

- Computer Assisted Instruction (CAI).

- Computer Based Learning (CBL).

Other terms are used, each of which carries its own abbreviation or acronym. Certainly more names will be used as more people invent techniques and still others use the systems. We'll use CAI when referring to the use of computers to present training materials.

The term Computer Managed Instruction (CMI) refers to the manipulation of learner data and, sometimes, the diagnostics and prescriptions. This term has been generally accepted, although the details of its meaning vary with different users and with different applications.

STATE-OF-THE-ART

The state-of-the-art and the marketplace are closely tied when considering the present condition of CAI. As the technology of the computers and their related equipment improve, the CAI techniques move another step forward. The development of the hardware outstrips the development of the CAI capability to take advantage of the new features.

Considerable work is being done today to take advantage of the technology, especially in the microprocessor field. The amount of work being done has been spurred on because microcomputers are in such widespread use. Until recently, schools couldn't afford to purchase their own computers, but with the microcomputers costing $1000 or less for a starter machine capable of providing CAI, there has been a virtual explosion of computers in schools, homes, and small businesses—places where they never were used before. Many more people are becoming conversant with computer terminology and use. "Computer literacy" is a term applied to one's understanding of these amazing machines. Computer literacy is in vogue today, and children at very young ages are being introduced to computers, often via games and other toy-like devices, some of which talk back.

Computers can take many forms; they can accept inputs from different sources; and they can communicate with the users in many ways. We usually think of a computer as represented by a keyboard and a video screen, or Cathode Ray Tube (CRT), but they can be in the form of games, such as the currently popular arcade games, the children's games, and feedback mechanisms such as those found in automobiles and biofeedback equipment. Computers are also used as switches to turn other devices on and off.

In a training application the computer can turn on a videotape machine at the proper time to present a lesson and then branch back to the CAI lesson presented to the learner via a voice synthesizer. The learner talks back to the computer via another device that translates the learner's voice into digital signals.

The computer also works as a communications link, and can be networked so that people in different parts of the world can participate in seminars without ever leaving the comfort of their homes or offices.

Finally, the computer has an excellent memory, and can keep track of everything that happens in all of these interactions, presentations, and communications. It can provide any information it has at the request of the learner. It's safe to say that, at this writing, the computer's state-of-the-art far surpasses the ability of trainers to take full advantage of it. The frontier is there—we need imaginative and creative explorers to push it back.

Hardware is the equipment, and the *software* is the collective programming that makes the hardware function as a computer. *Programming* is the process of instructing the computer hardware to

HARDWARE, SOFTWARE, AND COURSEWARE

perform specific functions. Computer systems are generally considered to come in three sizes:

1. Large scale mainframe installations require specially air-conditioned, humidity controlled environments and cost many hundreds of thousands of dollars and more. These computers are used by large organizations to perform routine processing on very large numbers of accounts or individual files. They are used by insurance companies, banks, large manufacturing organizations, most government agencies, and by time-sharing services, where many users have the opportunity to share the large capacity of the mainframe computer installation.

2. Minicomputer installations are scaled-down versions of the large-scale computers. Many minicomputer installations perform preliminary processing functions for the mainframe installations. They are usually in the price range of $100,000 to $300,000 and are used primarily in branch offices of large organizations. Some of the minicomputer installations are considered as independent stand-alone, self-contained systems that perform all the data processing and word processing for the organization.

3. Microcomputers require no special installation and may cost less than $100. They are based on a microprocessor chip about the size of a stick of chewing gum. This chip contains the logic to perform the processing of the computer. The microprocessors are virtually everywhere, including your wristwatch, calculator, automobile, microwave oven, or television set. The microcomputer, or personal computer, is a system made up of the microprocessor chip plus a set of input, output, and storage components.

Software is of several types. The distinctions between them can be important when considering training applications.

System software is made up of those programs that cause the machine to behave as a computer. It includes operating systems, compilers, and interpreters which are the communicators with the users. Each computer has system software that is unique to that machine, thereby making transfer of software from one machine to another difficult, if not impossible. Some types of software are transferable from one computer type to others, but even then, the transfer is not always without problems.

Applications software is made up of those programs that perform specific tasks that make use of the computer. Applications are added to the basic computer system software and are programs that work as accounting packages, communications subsystems, word processing functions, data management systems, and all the other programs that are designed to *make the computer useful.* These programs, too, are often not transferable from one computer to others, although some programs are. The programming that provides the capability to prepare CAI materials on the computer for presentation on the computer is an applications program.

Courseware is the material produced for use by the student and the administrator/instructor/monitor by the applications programs. The courseware is the data of the applications programs, containing only the intelligence put there by the author of the training. The paradigm is quite simple: A training developer, usually called an author, designs the training to be applied via CAI. Using the hardware to communicate with the applications programs, the author instructs the computer to produce materials to satisfy the design, thereby producing courseware.

Still other applications software establishes the capability of students to have access to the courseware and to monitor and control the presentation of the CAI. The CMI functions are performed by yet another set of applications programs. The actual software is transparent to the author and to the students. The newer authoring systems permit the author to prepare the training materials with little or no knowledge of the computer or its programming. The author can concentrate on the training, rather than on worrying about the workings of the computer.

Today software capability can produce courseware on virtually every computer on the market. The kinds of courseware and the ease of authoring vary widely for different equipment. Anyone planning to use CAI should perform a complete analysis of the need and then acquire the hardware and software necessary to produce the kinds of materials needed. Microprocessor hardware costs so little that any substantial training application could easily justify the purchase of the most suitable equipment. It is no longer necessary to fashion a makeshift patch to an existing large-scale computer that may not have the authoring software or other needed features.

Users

When we talk about CAI as another instructional medium, there is likely to be greater acceptance if we omit the word *"computer."* The word itself conjures up goblins to the very large numbers of people who are truly frightened of the idea of ever *touching* one of those mysterious marvels. Young children accept computers as naturally as they accept any other device they can manipulate. There are essentially no problems with getting the youngsters to accept the idea of learning from a machine. Their parents and their teachers, on the other hand, are not always prepared to overcome what may be a general mistrust of machines. There is also the concept of newness in the approach that many adults find difficult to accept, especially when considering such an approach for their children. In other adult training applications, there has been much greater general acceptance of CAI, but most adults who have had no previous exposure to computers are wary in their approach to using them.

Any CAI training program should include a gentle introduction to computers that leads the learner carefully into greater and greater acceptance of the approach. Care must be exercised to explain that the computer is "friendly" and is going to help make their lives better. We need to tell the learner in a CAI situation what records are being kept, and what is being done with those records. We need to build a trust and do nothing later to betray it. Now, many people still need that kind of reassurance and "hand-holding" to even begin to accept computers. The reputation of the computer in the general population is not a positive one. That is changing gradually, but people will be using the computers long before the acceptance is at a level to make that use as successful as it otherwise might be.

A good example of purposeful avoidance of the term *"computer"* in hopes of engendering greater user acceptance is evident in the term *"word processing."* Word processors are computers but they are introduced to the office as word processors, usually with no reference to the fact that the same machine is basically a computer. If you ask a word processor user in an office, "How do you like your computer?" you'll likely receive the response, "Oh, this isn't a computer. It's a word processor." If that same system were introduced as a computer, acceptance probably would have been much more difficult. In fact, there are people who have been introduced to word processing as a computer application and never thereafter could they be induced to even consider using the machine to prepare text materials. This is a phenomenon that we need to keep in mind when we discuss CAI with people who have little or no understanding of the techniques or power inherent in the method. Many people who are unfamiliar with computers fear that the machines are smarter than they are and will make them appear foolish or, worse, will somehow control their actions. These are real fears that we must deal with every time we approach a new CAI application.

Authors

The people who prepare the materials that become the CAI lessons used by learners are called authors. Each different CAI applications program requires different skills and knowledge of the author. The authors communicate with the computer program telling the computer what to do. This communication is accomplished by *author languages*. Author languages range in complexity and difficulty from very simple and easy to learn to very complex and time consuming to learn. The simple author languages require virtually no knowledge of the computer, while the more complex languages require a detailed understanding of the computer and the knowledge of some programming. The latter systems may require up to a year for an author to become proficient in their use, while the simpler ones require little or no familiarization time. The difficulty level and time required for learning to use the system should be considered when you select the kind of system to use.

Post-Authoring Production

Some CAI systems require preparation of the materials for use by the students, while some do not. This consideration influences time and cost, but has little or no impact on the presentation quality or learning effectiveness of the materials. It is simply another factor to consider when planning to implement a CAI system.

Presentation Flexibility

Two methods are used for getting the CAI materials to the learners:

1. Individual, dispersed units.
2. Centralized facilities.

In the dispersed unit configuration, terminals are located in convenient locations, including at workers' desks and the terminals where other work is being performed throughout the organization.

Where microcomputers are used, the learner may be permitted to take a computer home to complete the learning. Where the CAI is on a large-scale computer, the students may take a terminal to a convenient location, including their own homes, and communicate with the computer via their telephones. Some microcomputer systems have this kind of communications capability as well.

Still another method is the *network* presentation, where a number of "dumb" terminals are connected to a central computer containing the courseware. All types of computers can be connected in a network configuration. The network provides greater security and control for the administration of the training, an important factor in certain settings.

The ideal method for presenting CAI materials is as part of the system the user is learning. This method is generally called *embedded* training. The training is part of the system itself. For example, if the user uses a computer or terminal as part of the job that is being trained, the training is accomplished using the identical equipment and, where possible, the same software and data. Management information systems, accounting systems, word processing systems, and other computer-based systems lend themselves to the embedded training approach. If embedded training is used, it's almost essential that the training component be designed in conjunction with the system itself. Often, it's difficult, if not impossible, to convince the system designers that the training should be part of the basic system, but more systems are being designed as user friendly, where the user may request guidance or help throughout the process. The helpfulness is usually available upon request of the user, so that it won't interfere when it's not needed. As more systems incorporate the user learning requirements, additional training should become less of a requirement than it is today.

SUITABLE SUBJECT MATTER

As a general rule, it's safe to say that virtually any subject is grist for the CAI mill. This is especially true when manipulation of language or numbers is an important component. Skills requiring manipulation of other devices may be made part of a multimedia CAI program, with the computer providing the instruction and the feedback, and the other devices providing the actual practice. If the subject can be conceptualized and defined, it is probably appropriate for CAI presentation.

Testing

Some authors prefer to begin a CAI session with a diagnostic test to help determine the level of learner knowledge or skill. For example, if the author prepares a series of increasingly difficult mathematical problems, the computer can determine, from the learner's performance, at what point to begin the training. The same kind of testing can be performed, of course, without leading to a learning experience. The CAI technology lends itself very nicely to a variety of tests and for collecting survey data.

Drill and Practice

The computer is a patient teacher. It won't be bored by "dumb" questions, and is willing to repeat the same lessons forever. Probably the simplest form of presentation is drill and practice, where the computer presents the learner with a series of questions or problems and continues until the learner reaches a preestablished level of proficiency.

EXAMPLE:

1. Spell the word of the animal that catches mice. It rhymes with rat.

2. Which spelling, meaning the entire thing, is correct?
   A. hole
   B. hoal
   C. whole
   D. howl

3. Which of the following is spelled incorrectly?
   A. holy
   B. wholly
   C. holely
   D. holey

4. Which word in the following list is spelled correctly?
   A. embarass
   B. embarras
   C. embarrass
   D. embaras

The format of the questions may be varied. The computer contains the answers and can be set to give the learners feedback immediately, or wait until the entire test is completed. There may be occasions where the answers are not to be given to the learners, but the data are to be used for other purposes. The learner may be told by the computer that an answer is correct or incorrect, without giving the correct answer in the latter instance. In such situations, the author may wish simply to ask the learner to continue trying until the correct answer is found, or to provide the correct answer only after a preset number of failures. The computer keeps track of scores and performance on each item, which may or may not be made available to the learner, at the discretion of the designer or author.

Learner performance on the test or drill and practice sessions can be used to establish where the next learning segment is to begin. For example, drill and practice sessions on fractions can lead into portion planning as part of a cooking course. The learners will not be permitted to begin the portions training until they have demonstrated a specific level of proficiency using fractions. Thus, the test may be used as a diagnostic to determine the entry level of the learner, as a drill and practice device, and as a prescriptive, or preparation, tool.

Items of information that must be memorized, and process or serial kinds of information lend themselves particularly to CAI presentation. Drill and practice may be applied to complex and difficult subject matter, as well as to the basic skills.

Teach and Test

Teach and test describes the sequence where a presentation is followed by a series of questions about the materials presented. CAI is particularly well suited to the branching that develops from the results of the test. If the learner performs at a specified level, the program can branch to another lesson that advances the learner's understanding and knowledge. If the learner performs below a specified level, the program can branch back to the items missed on the test or to a parallel level of presentation. This kind of presentation and manipulation of information ensures that the learner will be dealing with the appropriate level of information at all times.

The teach and test method is really a variation of the classic classroom method; the major—and important—difference is that it is tailored to each learner on a dynamic basis. As the learner performs, the program modifies its presentation. This is the antithesis of the computer as a page turner, and is an essential distinction.

The manner in which the teach and test method is used depends upon the imagination and resourcefulness of the author. The computer will display the information as instructed. Most CAI systems include some graphics capability. The level of sophistication of the graphics varies widely; some are capable of animation and high resolution, while others are quite simple and primitive, with limited capacity for animation. Static line drawings are available on virtually all CAI systems. Again, the author's design tends to be the most limiting factor in the use of graphics. Since each system has its own graphics potential, the author should determine precisely how to make it perform as desired. In most systems, the graphics presentation can be mixed with text. Other graphics features include reversal of figure and ground, flashing characters, color, and movement.

THE FUTURE

The use of computers for training is moving rapidly along both parallel and converging paths. On one hand, the manufacturers of equipment containing microprocessors and designers of large-scale computer-based systems are building in the capability to instruct new users and to aid experienced users who may require assistance to perform functions that have been forgotten. These systems are the ones that incorporate the human factor considerations at the early design stages. They don't wait until the system is designed and built and then design training to accommodate the human performance design deficiencies. The embedded training design is becoming more prevalent. Large companies producing these systems are aware of the ever-increasing costs surrounding additional training and are aware that their products sell better if they're user friendly.

On the other hand, we have large numbers of existing training requirements that are not on computer-based systems. These are by far the most common today, and the ones where the external CAI system is being applied increasingly. Whenever a substantial number of people need to be trained on the same material, it is faster, cheaper, and frequently more effective to use CAI materials that have been developed by experts and tested to establish their efficacy. More and more publishers will be distributing CAI course materials for use on home computers and for commercial and business applications. They are being used more in government and military installations because they're effective and the costs are reasonable.

The future will see a trend toward far greater application of computers in training and in education. It has been estimated that by 1990 more than 90 percent of all industrial training will be supported by CAI. While that estimate may be high, the trend is clear. As the technology for two-way voice communications is developed and refined, the computer's popularity and application in training will increase. Voice communication will tend to remove the remaining vestiges of resistance to the machines.

As more young people are introduced to educational computer toys, there will be more and more acceptance of the concept and computers will be accepted more widely in the relatively near future.

19

Estimating Costs

Costs associated with the development and delivery of training programs are:

- Labor.
- Materials and supplies, including publishing.
- Travel and subsistence.

The principal monetary cost usually is associated with labor. Time is a cost factor that is most often reflected in the labor costs, although calendar time and the numbers of people working on a project cannot always be traded one for the other. For example, if more people with shovels and strong backs are added to the crew digging a ditch, the ditch will be dug faster, all other things being equal. However, in training development, adding people to the program development often has little or no positive impact on the development schedule.

Cost questions always arise when considering training program development. The sponsor needs to be able to budget resources to

151

ensure successful completion of the program. Therefore, the training developer must be able to provide a reasonably accurate estimate of the costs associated with each phase of the development process, and for the total costs to the point where the program has been tested and is ready for learners. Schedule information, of necessity, accompanies the cost information.

Many factors influence training program costs. Media and materials costs may vary extravagantly from one program to another. Some programs require more extensive data collection and analysis than others, while still others accrue large publishing costs.

A Typical Example

While all training programs are different, some are more different than others, but, like fingerprints, they all have some unique features. With that in mind, let's consider a "typical" example.

The typical training program will follow the training development process, beginning with a task analysis, followed by developing the training requirements, objectives, criterion test materials, and the trainee's and instructor's materials. The typical program will be presented by an instructor or might be self-administered.

There are several key variables in the typical example. They have a substantial impact on the overall program cost. First, training for an existing application costs far less than one that is being used for the first time. It's less costly to develop a training program to teach typing or bricklaying than it is to do so for a system that is in the process of development. Therefore, the typical example assumes that the application is an existing one.

A second factor that influences cost significantly is the availability of a subject-matter expert (SME). A SME is a person who can translate the requirements and task data to practical reality and steer the development along a true course. Often the SME can provide so much of the task analysis and requirements data that those development phases require less effort than would otherwise be the case. The SME can preclude false starts and be of considerable help through the development process.

Keep in mind that although there is really no typical training development, there is the typical process. The steps in the process should be performed in all cases. The degree to which they will be accomplished varies with the subject matter and the kind of sponsor support that's made available.

The first activity of the training developer is the "get smart" investigation. Training developers are often extremely fast learners, or "quick studies." If the training developer is completely unfamiliar with the subject, the get smart period is, of course, longer than if there is some existing knowledge. In any case, the training developer may require time to adapt existing knowledge to the specific application to be trained. For example, the training developer may be familiar with the subject, but not with the people who are to be trained, nor with the training environment. All relevant aspects of the program need to be examined.

In some cases, it's quite simple to define the subject matter and spend very little time investigating the other aspects. Such may be the case when you're preparing a new employee orientation for a large organization. You can safely assume that the new employees know very little, if anything, about the organization, and you know the requirements for employment, so you can deduce the educational levels of the employees, their special skills, and other relevant factors. If the orientation is designed to convey the organization's benefits program, the investigation may simply involve reading policies and other materials that already exist in the organization, and supplementing this information with interview data acquired from subject-matter experts in the organization.

A simpler instance might be developing a basic accounting program, using a specific text as the information base.

If the developer knows anything about accounting, the initial get smart phase can be very short. Even if the developer knows very little about accounting, the task is largely one of converting from one medium (a textbook) to another (a set of lecture notes or a self-administered program).

The get smart phase, therefore, usually consumes anywhere from virtually no time to several weeks. If the training is for a complex system that is still in the process of being designed, the costs will be substantial, sometimes requiring many months or years for the initial phase. Estimation of costs for this phase essentially depends upon:

- Subject-matter expert support.
- Whether the subject to be trained is an existing one or is still being designed.
- The complexity and difficulty of the subject.
- Available information about the people to be trained (target population).
- The numbers of training developers that can effectively perform the investigation.
- Reasonableness of the schedule.

The rule of thumb for estimating the labor costs for a full-blown development, following the process defined earlier, is roughly forty labor hours of development time for each hour of training time.

Using the 40-to-1 ratio is for guidance only. There are circumstances which make this estimate too high, while under different conditions, it is too low. Whether numbers are added or subtracted depends on many variables, but the following should narrow the range somewhat:

- If one person is performing the entire program development, there is less need for coordination and no time is spent in time-consuming meetings and in waiting for others to complete their work. It is reasonable to reduce the estimate under such conditions by as much as one-fourth to one-third.

- If the training developer is also the subject-matter expert, the estimate can be adjusted again by as much as one-fourth, since the research in such a case is minimal.

- If an existing program can be modified to suit the needs established for this program, the development time may be reduced accordingly.

- If a substantial amount of material to be used in the course is already developed and produced, the cost estimates can again be reduced accordingly. Prepared materials include audiovisual presentations such as films and videotapes, and readings prescribed from books, periodicals, or other materials.

- Inclusion of time-consuming activities such as visits, guest speakers, extended practice sessions, and others that require little or no developer preparation time will, of course, further reduce the labor costs for development.

- Study periods and group discussions should be eliminated from the total hours of program time used for cost estimating.

Consider the following—a planned forty-hour course that's designed to include:

- A half-day visit to a construction site, where the trainees will collect information using a checklist provided by the instructor.

- Three guest lecturers, who have been invited to speak for two hours each on their areas of expertise and, therefore, require no development time from the training developer.

- Two three-hour laboratory sessions where the trainees will experiment with their designs developed during the course.

- Twenty-minute presentations by each trainee of the results of their experiments. Twelve trainees will be in the program.

Thus, sixteen hours may be subtracted from the forty-hour program, leaving twenty-four hours of development cost remaining. Based on the 40-to-1 ratio, we would estimate 960 labor hours for development of this program. If we had ignored the factors listed above, the estimate would have been 1600 labor hours.

Another factor is difficult to specify or to quantify, but a phenomenon in training development is that only the simplest of programs can take less than three calendar months to complete. At the same time, the range of complexity and difficulty that can be accomplished in a three-month period is sometimes amazing. You just determined that the forty-hour course defined earlier probably would require about twenty-four hours of materials, or 960 hours of development time. The 960 hours is equivalent to approximately six months. If one person were to develop this program, chances are it could be accomplished in less than the twenty-four weeks projected, and perhaps could be completed in twelve to fifteen weeks if conditions were ideal and Murphy's Law took a holiday.

If all this appears to indicate that cost estimation for training development is less than precise, you may be drawing a valid conclusion. Experience will be a better teacher, but some rule of thumb estimate can at least put a bracket around reasonable expectations.

In practice, there are more factors that *lengthen* the development process than shorten it. The most common and devastating are the *changes* that almost always are decided upon *after the bulk of the work is done*. Some elements of the work require considerably more than the 40-to-1 ratio suggests. Unexpected and often unwanted interruptions in the flow of input to the development are common and lengthen the time to develop the program by varying amounts, depending on the extent and duration of the interruption, as well as the point in the development cycle at which it occurs. Generally, the earlier in the development cycle the changes are made, the less the impact on the costs, since less work will need to be redone as a result of the changes.

Rules of thumb, by definition, are imprecise estimating tools. Unless highly unusual circumstances affect the program development, the 40-to-1 rule has proven reasonably reliable. There are occasions when the costs will approximate 20-to-1, while other programs conceivably could result in an 80-to-1 ratio. The latter figure most often is the result of a catastrophic event or series of events that caused extensive delays or redesign of most of the program.

The most efficient program design is performed by a single training developer. Adding more people usually results in higher costs and lowered productivity. However, when programs are lengthy and content is varied, numbers of training developers may be required to work in parallel so that the program can be completed in a reasonable time. Under such circumstances, it's far better to assign discrete modules to each developer so they may work independently.

Under such conditions, the training program requires project management application. A project manager (or coordinator) establishes assignments, schedules, formats, reviews, and technical checkpoints. The project manager ensures that the resulting training program meets the design specification and satisfies the goals and objectives set forth in the initial design.

If the project includes two to four people, the project manager often performs a training development function in addition to the management duties.

An effectively managed program of the type described here will often be completed within the 40-to-1 estimate, including the costs for the manager's time, especially if the manager shares in the development activities.

Another effective method of keeping costs down is to have periodic progress reviews with the program sponsor or user. The reviews should be planned ahead and taken seriously by all parties. They should be frequent enough so that the sponsor/user won't spend an undue amount of time preparing for the review, but they should not be so frequent that they disrupt the development activity. *Work should not stop while waiting for the results of a review.* On a program of three months or longer, biweekly reviews are appropriate. Results of the reviews should be documented, even if the report of the review is a penciled note. The report provides a communication device for other interested parties, but more importantly, it provides a memo for the developer and the sponsor to refer to when a question arises.

Continuity of personnel is a vital factor when a project of this type is established. If the sponsor/user changes during the development cycle, extensive changes can be expected. Changing the project manager is often less critical, although changing the program developer in mid-course could be disastrous. Unless the program is very large, building in redundancy and backup capacity most often doesn't work. If a training developer leaves the project part-way through the development, someone else will need to complete the work. The project manager should encourage the newly assigned person to complete the work, following the plan and accepting the work already completed. This is usually possible if the ground rules were established at the beginning.

There can be as many kinds of presentations as there are people designing and delivering them. But the different kinds of presentations can, fortunately, be classified and recognized. Some of the distinctions may be somewhat arbitrary, but they are useful for estimating program development costs.

We have already discussed the 40-to-1 rule of thumb for cost estimating. That rule of thumb is applicable to most written materials, whether they're lecture notes, detailed scripted instructions, or even programmed instruction. The rule assumes that the developer is experienced and reasonably proficient in the development process. If the developers are inexperienced the 40-to-1 rule won't hold.

The significant costs are incurred when using audiovisual media, particularly videotape, film, and videodisk. These require extensive expert assistance and a wide range of expensive technical equipment. Many people new to the field believe that having used a camera at some point in one's life qualifies them as experts in the production of audiovisual materials. Unfortunately, such is not the case. This is one time that it truly pays to use experts. Many organizations have invested hundreds of thousands of dollars in the latest, most sophisticated equipment to produce audiovisual materials. Most of them have regretted that investment because the facility couldn't attract or retain the quality of professional talent necessary to produce the kinds of materials needed.

The cost estimates for audiovisual materials are based on the use of professional support. If, for example, we're costing a film, we include a scriptwriter, a director, at least one technician, and studio time costs. The same would be true if we were considering videotape or videodisk.

Costs for initial production of audiovisual materials are many times higher than for written materials. For that reason alone, the decision to produce them should be carefully considered. The cost for changing these kinds of materials after they have been completed is also very high, so stable material should be selected, as well as material that is to be presented to large numbers of people over a broad geographical area or at intervals in a few locations. Copies of audiovisual materials are more expensive than copies of paper materials.

Cost estimating rules of thumb for audiovisual materials vary more with the reputation of the vendor preparing them than with the costs for materials and facilities. Using the 1982 dollar, professional production costs for videotape, film, or videodisk are similar, about $1,000 per minute of finished presentation—*to the production organization.*

If the finished product is ten to sixty minutes long, the rule of thumb is reasonably accurate. If the final product is less than ten minutes in length, the cost per minute may be as high as $1500, because of setup time and other fixed costs that can't be spread over a longer production.

Equipment for the presentation of the finished audiovisual materials is not included in these cost estimates. If the equipment already exists in the organization, there is little additional cost. However, if the equipment needs to be acquired, those costs must be added to the training program costs.

Another set of cost factors that is often overlooked when considering use of these media is the required lead times, the labor involved in working with the production people, and the actual production time.

The decision to include these kinds of audiovisuals in a training program should be taken seriously and made only if the costs can be justified to higher levels of management. Making large investments in materials that can't be completely justified can do more harm to your organization than development of an otherwise unimpressive training program that has far less visibility and exposure for the developer. Remember, these kinds of visual presentations are subject to interpretation, and you can expect some people to think they are a waste of time and money, even if others think they are worth every penny. The cost of an already expensive program may include the career of the program developer, as well.

Other audiovisual materials carry far less investment. Full color 35mm slides generally cost about $50, using the 1982 dollar as a base. If the artwork is finished and provided, the cost is far less. The graphic arts costs vary, depending on the content of the slide. If the slide contains only words, the cost may be as low as $15, while "exotic" art may cost more than $100. If professional models or fine artists are involved, their rates need to be added to the base costs.

The costs for the developers' time required to coordinate and prepare the ideas for the artists is not included in these estimates. They may be extra, or may be included in the 40-to-1 rule.

Overhead slides usually can be prepared with minimum lead time and can be quite complex, with overlays and colors. The costs for these kinds of materials are similar to those for 35mm slides, but can be lower for simple verbal slides and line drawings. Overhead slides can be made from printed materials, using xerographic copiers. These are probably the least expensive of the audiovisual presentations and are the easiest to change.

Slide-tape presentations are sound-coordinated 35mm slides that use a specially designed projection system to deliver the sound and the pictures simultaneously, as in a sound film. These presentations are prepared on separate slides and tapes, making them relatively independent. Changing the slide-tape programs is not as costly as some other audiovisual materials, but is time-consuming and subject to errors. Changing the sequence of slides requires rework of the audio segment—usually a new recording, although editing and splicing may be possible under some conditions.

Music is often desired for background on slide-tape presentations. Sometimes royalties must be paid for the rights to use the music selected. Even if the music is in the public domain, costs for its acquisition can be expected. Use of music on the slide-tape makes later editing virtually impossible. Altogether, a slide-tape costs about one-tenth the cost of a videotape, film, or videodisk presentation.

This section discusses the printed materials and adjunctive aids that are used in virtually every training program, including those that rely heavily on audiovisual materials.

Trainee Materials

The costs for the printed materials are preponderantly for the trainee's materials. The instructor's materials may use most of the development cost for a training program, but the trainee's materials almost always cost more to produce.

The trainee's materials are generally made more attractive than the instructor's materials, and may be housed in colorful binders and printed on multicolor pages of high quality paper stock.

Printing costs vary widely, depending on the quality of the paper, the printing method, and the number of colors. The most significant factor in determining printing costs is the *run size*. Unit costs for small runs can be several times more expensive than for large runs. The definition of large and small runs is a matter to discuss with printers. Competition among printers is often keen, thus getting several bids from reputable printers can often result in considerable savings.

It can be a severe blow to a training developer to learn, late in the development cycle, that the budget includes everything except the preparation of the materials that will be the ultimate learning vehicle for the trainees. *Printing costs can be substantial and should be considered in the early project planning.*

Rules of thumb for estimating printing are, by 1982 standards, about ten cents per page. While the number will vary, the ten cents per page figure should give an outside estimate for quality printing, including printed binders and multicolor printing for larger runs. For smaller runs, the ten cents per page estimate is for black-and-white production and simply printed binders.

A simple estimating formula for printing costs is:

$$\text{Printing Cost (C)} = .1 \, (P \times S), \text{ where}$$

P = Number of *pages* per set of materials.
S = Number of *sets* to be produced.

Training Aids and Job Aids

The training developer frequently designs items to aid trainee learning and performance on the job. These training and job aids may range from simple notes to elaborate templates, tools, or other manufactured items. Costs for these aids must be considered when budgeting the program. The costs for aids can be substantial and, as for printing, run length is an important cost determinant.

Training aids are used *during* the training, while the job aids are used *after* the training has been completed. Learners use the training aids until they are able to perform without them. Job aids are often used on the job indefinitely. Job aids, therefore, are almost always made of durable materials. If the job aids are made of paper, they will often be laminated for protection and longer life. Training aids are used by each trainee for briefer periods of time and are often less durable than the job aids. However, if training aids are to be used by successive classes, then they, too, should be of more durable construction.

Certificates

One of the benefits of any training program is the recognition for accomplishment, represented by a certificate, plaque, or other visible device that the trainees may display at their work locations. Trainees often denigrate these tokens, but most people display them conspicuously. Course completion awards are of many types—from simple paper forms, signed by an instructor or administrator, to elaborate wood, metal, or plastic devices that are both attractive and expensive. Costs can range from virtually nothing to many dollars each. The decision to spend large sums for certificates depends, in part, on the numbers to be awarded, the importance placed on the program, and, of course the resources of the organization. While it may seem unfair, an expensive or ostentatious award for course completion would be inappropriate for a government employees' course, while it might be perfectly acceptable for a similar program for corporate executives.

PROGRAM LIFE EXPECTANCY

Changing technology and needs of the population create constant change to training requirements. Fads and styles also require changes to training programs. The life expectancy of a training program also is determined by how many people need to be trained, and over what period of time. Personnel turnover rates contribute to the duration of training programs.

Aside from the obsolescence created by changes to the substance of the subjects being trained, more subtle factors shorten the potential life of training programs. Audiovisual materials are especially sensitive to the passing of time because they reflect styles and tastes and become dated rapidly. Clothing styles change rapidly, as do automobiles and furniture. Even color combinations are in and out of vogue rapidly. Trainees are sensitive to the materials they use and resist anything that appears dated. Everyone wants to learn the latest, not something that's passé or that they might have seen last year. *Few specially built training programs survive the application to the original target population unchanged.*

When estimating costs per trainee for a training program, it's generally a good practice to consider only those trainees known to be candidates at the time of preparation. It usually is not safe to project application of the program to the general population or to unidentified learners. Most programs developed for a specific audience do not lend themselves to generic use. Projecting costs based on some unidentified target population is difficult to justify to the buyer of the training program.

PROGRAM MAINTENANCE

An effective method of extending the useful life of training programs is *keeping them up to date.* Many buyers of training programs neglect to include a budget for maintaining the program beyond its initial application. Learners are, understandably, very sensitive to errors or inconsistencies in their training materials. Training loses effectiveness rapidly when the students become aware that the program is out of date. It's far less costly to maintain a training program than it is to redo it completely because it has become dated.

Maintenance is essential if costs are a factor and if the program will be continued over a period of time where changes are expected. Training program maintenance is needed most where the initial development costs have been high, but especially where the subject matter is in continual flux. The training developer needs to be sensitive to the degree of volatility inherent in the material.

20

Training Trainers

"Anyone can teach" is a commonly heard phrase. The truth is that not anyone can teach—unless they are trained to do so. Of course, there are "naturals," but they are relatively rare and they, too, often benefit from training in the fine points.

This book is oriented toward creating training materials that can succeed either without an instructor or can help an instructor present the training. The early chapters stress the techniques for developing training materials that can provide learners with the skills and knowledge they need—with or without dependence upon instructors. Instructors may be necessary under certain conditions to provide feedback, human contact, a communications link, and an information source, among other things, while in other instances, instructors may not be required at all.

When an instructor is required for a training program, that person should have a comprehensive understanding of the training materials, the subject matter, and the techniques necessary for effective presentation of the materials. The roles of the instructors can vary widely, depending upon the training developer's design for the instructor. Typical roles for the instructor are:

- Traditional lecturer.

- Administrator.

- Facilitator.

- Expert.

- Feedback provider.

An instructor may assume all the roles in a single program or session, or may rely solely on one for a training program. This chapter addresses the different roles played by instructors in different types of training programs.

The traditional instructor is the wizened scholar or expert, whose age and reputation create an aura of respect and credibility. Credibility is a vital ingredient in instructor effectiveness. If the learners believe the instructor doesn't know the subject, the willingness to accept the words of the instructor is diminished.

Traditionally, the trainer or teacher is the expert. This is a long tradition, going back to the beginnings of history, through the Greek philosophers, through the longstanding apprenticeships and the guild system, to the present.

Today's world has become increasingly specialized, to a point where there aren't enough experts to meet the needs of all the people to learn. Moreover, the experts often have neither the time, the skills, nor the inclination to teach or to train others. There is a need to train people rapidly to perform tasks that must be accomplished competently and with minimum cost in time and money. In industry and government, these needs are becoming more keenly felt as world competition for markets and technology increases and the search for improved productivity intensifies.

The result is an ever-increasing demand for effective training in a world where people demand consideration and respect for their human and individual rights. Organizations need effective training to compete and to survive, while the workers and managers need the training to satisfy their individual needs. Trainers have had to become more efficient and more effective to satisfy the needs of the organizations and of the individuals.

While it's clearly impossible to have everyone trained by the expert in any field, it is possible for trainers to use the knowledge and techniques of the masters. Thus, training of trainers today includes a large portion of the concepts and techniques presented in Part 2 of this book, with particular emphasis on the meaning and application of learning objectives and criterion testing.

It's often necessary to find instructors who may not be expert in the subject matter, but who are capable of presenting materials well by following a set of well prepared materials. Large organizations find this to be increasingly effective. In many ways, these instructors are similar to actors, playing roles that they have studied and with which they have become comfortable.

Trainer training, therefore, must include the entire array of activities from classroom demeanor to discipline. It's not the task of this book to repeat those time-honored methods and techniques. Rather, we need to address those additional qualities that must be developed in the trainer of today, and to select from among them the ones that require particular emphasis.

Formal trainer training generally takes a threefold course:

- Training principles and practices.
- Techniques of classroom behavior.
- Observation and practice in the classroom.

Before the new instructor enters the classroom as certified, two assumptions must be made. The first is that the instructor has been provided with fully tested and complete training materials developed according to the principles and methods detailed in the early chapters of this book. The second assumption is that the instructor is qualified in the techniques of classroom presentation, including how to make the trainees comfortable and how to create an atmosphere conducive to learning. Instructors who will be following the prescribed program will deviate very little from the materials as they have been prepared. They will deal with all relevant trainee questions and will be responsive to the expressed and perceived needs of the learners.

Course administrators differ from instructors in the classroom in that they are responsible for assisting learners by answering questions, providing materials, administering and scoring tests, and being available to serve the needs of the learners who, in these kinds of classroom situations, are performing self-administered or self-paced lessons.

The training that requires the presence of a course administrator is usually solitary or involves small group activities, such as in a shop or laboratory, where the trainees actually produce or prepare something.

The course administrators are familiar with the materials and the procedures specified for the program, but do not usually lecture or teach in the traditional sense. Since there may be no instructor in the program, the materials provided to the learners and to the course administrator must be specific and clear. The materials prepared by the training developer, therefore, must include a course administrator's manual that contains learning objectives, criterion information, an hour-by-hour schedule of activities for which the course administrator is responsible or which the course administrator must perform.

Training for course administrators includes the same activities as for instructors, but there is less need to practice the actual lecture techniques, since they are not part of the course administrator's job. Training for course administrators usually consumes less time than that required for instructors.

PROGRAM FACILITATORS

Facilitators are instructors who function more as group leaders than traditional teachers. Facilitators usually don't lecture. Rather, they lead discussions and pose questions and problems for the trainees. They help keep discussions on course, and generally maintain the focus of activities. Often, there may be two or more facilitators in a program at any time, to work with subgroups.

Facilitators are used mostly in seminar or workshop settings, where the trainees are expected to develop interactive skills with others. It's important that the facilitators understand their roles and refrain from the temptation to offer too much assistance in the solution of problems. The ideal facilitator *guides* the group to *its* solution, not the facilitator's.

Training of facilitators is accomplished by carefully explaining the rules, as outlined above, and having them observe experienced, effective facilitators in the classroom. Facilitators in training should be exposed to other facilitators who are considered good, and be encouraged to ask them questions about why they did or said certain things. Facilitators may require longer training periods than instructors, since they need to know what the instructor may know, plus a broad knowledge of the subject. Facilitators may be expected to answer any relevant question in the classroom.

One important thing facilitators must learn is to say, "I don't know the answer to that question, but I'll try to get the answer for you." Facilitators should not be afraid to say that, especially after they have tried to elicit the answer from others in the class. Often the question can be resolved with the resources in the classroom—the other trainees.

HOTLINES

A hotline is most often a telephone used to reach an expert who can answer questions or help solve problems. The people at the receiving end of the hotline are usually expert in the subject for which the hotline is established. For example, if a new procedure is established in the organization and is to be implemented on a nationwide basis at the same time, it's impossible for the person who prepared the procedure to be in all those places at once, but it is possible to have that expert at the other end of a telephone to answer questions. Often, hotlines are established to support a large force of technicians who may need assistance in solving complex technical problems.

Hotlines are established more in the latter instance, where an on-going need exists. Training the experts in hotline instruction involves trying to get the callers to understand how the experts solved the problems. If the experts simply answer the questions, the same kinds of calls will continue. If, on the other hand, the expert explains how the solution is found, the caller may be able to solve similar problems in the future without calling the hotline.

The hotline expert is ideally an instructor who can lead the caller to a solution. Of course, all hotline calls don't lend themselves to a training solution, some require assistance of other types, such as helping to obtain an elusive part.

The training of the hotline expert is relatively simple—encourage the expert to work with the caller to define the problem with as much precision as possible, and then work with the caller to solve the problem, using as much of the caller's knowledge as possible. The expert should encourage the callers to use reference materials and to offer to send any references that might be relevant.

FEEDBACK

Just about everyone would agree that a person shooting a rifle at a target cannot make corrections in aiming unless there is knowledge of the results of where the previous round hit—or missed. A shooter can adjust aim based on the feedback of information. In the same way, learning in other areas benefits from feedback.

If a technician tunes an engine, sophisticated electronic equipment provides some of the information the technician needs. The technician also receives other forms of feedback, such as listening to the sound of the engine, operating the vehicle, and asking the customer for a reaction.

Adjustments to behavior may be used for feedback. All senses may be used for feedback. Vision, hearing, smell, touch, and taste are all used under different circumstances, depending on the activity. Instructors, facilitators, and any other people who assume roles of trainers must be aware of the importance of feedback to training and how and when to provide that essential feedback.

Feedback should occur as close to the event as possible—immediately, unless otherwise indicated. The impact of delayed feedback is about as useful as opening the umbrella after the rain stops. When a singer hits a wrong note, it should be pointed out. When the technician pushes the wrong button, the error should be recognized on the spot. When the student driver rides the clutch, the correction should be made at the time. People forget what they did when they made the incorrect response. As more time passes the impact of the feedback is lessened.

Trainers must be taught the methods used for providing feedback. In a simple stimulus-response situation, such as in the target example, the feedback method is simple. The learner is told where the round went. In a more complex problem-solving situation where the correct answers may not be so apparent, feedback deals more with process than with the substance of the decision. Trainers need to learn how to draw out the learner so that the process becomes clear to the trainee; the questions asked by the trainer may be tantamount to feedback.

The trainer must suppress value judgments in giving feedback. Feedback must be objective, unless the task is to please another person. In such cases, the other person tells the learner how well the action was liked and, to be most meaningful to the learner, why.

21

Training Evaluation

Training doesn't always work, and when it does, it's rarely 100 percent effective. Performance deficiencies don't always respond to training. Sometimes the skill required to do the job is impossible for the target population; sometimes the organization will not permit performance of the job as specified. There are many reasons why the solution to a performance problem may not be training. Sometimes there are design deficiencies inherent in the equipment that are so severe that no reasonable amount of training and learning can make the equipment usable or maintainable. These are all factors that must be considered when evaluating a training program.

Evaluation of training is perhaps the most misunderstood aspect of the entire process. We are so used to the traditional school approach of evaluating the *students* that it is difficult to suspect that the training itself might be faulty. This obstacle is being overcome in some sectors, but requires much greater understanding and a shift in emphasis from our usual way of thinking.

Part of the problem lies in the essential difference between education and training. Without getting into a philosophical discourse, the primary goal of education is to prepare students for their future lives, mainly by encouraging them to think and otherwise use their natural talents. Training, on the other hand, is oriented toward a more immediate payoff—when a trainee completes a program, that person is expected to be able to meet the objectives of the training, to perform a specific set of tasks to a specified criterion level.

We tend to assess the effectiveness of our educational programs by examining the "success" rate of graduates from our universities and other learning institutions, while we evaluate training programs by measuring the programs themselves, even while they are being conducted. Only later do we look at the activities of the people who complete the training. When we look at the people, we are asking if the training provided the necessary skills. This chapter discusses evaluation of training—its effectiveness in meeting its objectives, and the validity of those objectives.

While the number of possible evaluation criteria could be very large, it's necessary to narrow the list to those that are most needed and meaningful.

The measures considered most meaningful and essential are those relating to:

- Trainee acceptance.

- Appropriateness to the trainee population.

- Objectives assessment and job relevance.

Each of those measures requires a different technique for assessment. We'll examine each one separately.

TRAINEE ACCEPTANCE

Perhaps the least valid of all measures of training program effectiveness is the trainee's reaction to the materials and to the presentation. Trainees tend to be more impressed with the presentation than with the substance of the program. About all that can be learned from asking the trainees for their reactions to a training program is whether they liked it or not. Expect no significant correlation between trainees' statements of like or dislike and the measured effectiveness of the program.

Trainee reactions to a program can influence their learning, however, and if reactions are sufficiently negative, learning may be minimal. Dealing with this issue requires considerable care and analysis. For example, trainees rarely like military basic training, but how does that affect their learning or meeting the learning objectives? On the other hand, if a newly hired office worker is trained using the same military training approach, the results may be far less positive. The conditions under which the training is administered may be more influential than the particular training methods used. Sometimes the environmental conditions, such as noise and temperature, have more impact on the trainees than the approach. However, the trainees generally react to these factors as though they were part of the training; they can have negative reactions toward the course when, in reality, the distraction of the nearby airport was the major contributor to their negative reactions.

Despite the frequently low validity and questionable value to the course developer or program administrator, it's usually advisable to collect trainee comments on a program for several reasons:

- It alerts the course administrator, course developer, and instructors to potentially serious problems. For example, if a large number of trainees complain that a particular module is unclear, it should lead to a reassessment of that module.

- It provides the trainees with an "official" vehicle of expression. Besides allowing the trainees to "let off steam," they sometimes provide usable information for program revision.

- It can provide data that can be correlated with longitudinal data, such as performance on the job or in subsequent training. If, for example, a module is reported as not seeming to be relevant to the job, and data collected on the job demonstrates that the subject matter of that module is, indeed, not applicable to the job, then course revision may be appropriate.

While the trainees' critiques may be oral or written, it's better to ask the trainees to complete a form. A written form has more credibility than notes made by an instructor or course administrator. It may be advisable to discuss the completed forms in class under certain circumstances, but that may not be possible in all cases, such as when the course is self-administered at remote and separate locations.

The Module Assessment Report is an example of the type of end of module or end of course evaluation requested of trainees. Note that the *appearance* of objectivity can be enhanced by asking the trainees to rate each item on a five-point scale. The difference between a three and a four may be completely meaningless, while one trainee's three may be equivalent to another's five. Only if almost all trainees rate an item very high or very low is it usually worth the developer's attention.

APPROPRIATENESS TO POPULATION

If the training materials, content, or subject matter are beyond the ability of the trainees to understand, then clearly, there has been a mismatch that must be corrected. One of the first steps in the development process is to determine the characteristics of the target population. Even though this step may be carried out, on occasion, the developer misses one or more estimates of the existing skill or knowl-

COURSE: _____ MODULE: _____ DATE: _____

NAME: _____ LOCATION: _____

ORGANIZATION: _____

Please circle the number that best expresses how you rate the following, on a scale of 1–5 (5 is best):

1. Overall assessment of the module   1 2 3 4 5

2. Relevance of the module to the job   1 2 3 4 5

3. Clarity of the materials   1 2 3 4 5

4. Interest level of the materials   1 2 3 4 5

5. Difficulty of the materials   1 2 3 4 5

6. Accuracy of the materials   1 2 3 4 5

7. Degree of confidence in performing the activities
   learned in the module   1 2 3 4 5

8. What did you like most about the module? _____
   _____

9. What did you like least about the module? _____
   _____

10. What changes would you recommend? _____
    _____

11. Please make any other comments you feel might be useful to the
    training program developers. _____
    _____
    _____
    _____
    _____

edge. There are instances where the definition of the target population is vague, leading the developers to be too broad in their definition of entering skills and knowledge. This often happens in military organizations and in public school systems, where the range of abilities is large and the details are unknown until the trainee group is in place.

Determination of the appropriateness of the training to the target population may be accomplished in several ways, any or all of which may be applied to a program.

In a classroom, the instructor is often a good judge of whether the training is at the right level and has the appropriate content for the group. Instructor judgment may be supplemented by an observer who is checking for behavior such as:

- An unusually high number of questions.

- Statements that suggest the trainees have insufficient background to deal with the material successfully.

- Unusual amounts of squirming, sleeping, talking, reading, and general discomfort or boredom.

The Training Assessment Form can serve as a guide for the instructor or observer to assess the appropriateness of the training to the class.

When the training is self-administered outside a classroom, and no instructor or observer is present, it is more difficult to assess the appropriateness of the material to the individual. However, trainees in self-study programs should have access to counselors with whom they can discuss problems and provide feedback relative to the appropriateness of the training. The Training Assessment Form can be used as a guide for the counselor when discussing the training with the trainee.

Another method for assessing the appropriateness of the training is to have assessment forms completed by the trainees at the end of each training segment or module. The Module Assessment Report may be modified to collect the information.

Sometimes the inappropriateness of the training is so dramatically demonstrated that it's difficult to believe any analysis of the target population was carried out in the first place. Even with a thorough analysis, it's not too surprising to find we've missed the mark. The time between definition of the target population and the time when the program is administered may be many months, or even years. The world keeps changing, and the original group designated as trainees for the program may have changed and an entirely different group may be presented for training. Whenever possible, the developer should remain aware of changes of this type, but sometimes the changes are made without knowledge of the training developer.

TRAINING ASSESSMENT FORM

COURSE: _____ MODULE: _____

Circle the number that best expresses how you rate each of the following, on the 5-point scale (5 is high):

1. Trainee comfort with the material   1 2 3 4 5

2. Instructor comfort level   1 2 3 4 5

3. Overall estimate of appropriateness   1 2 3 4 5

4. Details of presentation (overall):   1 2 3 4 5

    a. Language used   1 2 3 4 5

    b. Visuals used   1 2 3 4 5

    c. Exercise materials used   1 2 3 4 5

Note: If more than two items are scored below 3, closer examination is recommended.

An even worse situation arises when the target population is defined as uniform and homogeneous in composition, yet appears in the class as a completely heterogeneous sample. These are facts of life with which trainers are forced to live. It's also one reason that trainers often spend many moonlight hours revising the program at the last moment. Once the trainees are in class, they expect to be trained, and the administration expects that the systematically developed program is exactly what is needed. Often, unfortunately, such is not the case. The sooner we recognize the problems that exist in the training, the sooner they can be corrected and the more successful the training can be.

Measurement of achievement of objectives is a relatively simple matter, if the objectives are stated completely and if the criterion test items are truly testing the behavior identified in the objectives. There are big "ifs" in that statement. Objectives and criterion test items often appear to be reasonable, accurate, and complete, but still don't quite do the job. For example, if we have as an objective that the trainee will be able to recite the Greek alphabet in thirty seconds without error, we can measure that behavior by asking the trainee to recite the Greek alphabet while we hold a stopwatch. We can observe and measure the behavior quite easily, assuming that the person administering the test knows the Greek alphabet.

But what if the reason for learning the Greek alphabet is because the trainee is going to be performing activities requiring mathematical formulas that incorporate Greek letters? If that were the case, perhaps the objective itself is inappropriate, since simply being able to recite the Greek alphabet doesn't ensure that the trainee can recognize the letters in a mathematical formula. Even worse, there is no indication that the trainee will understand the meaning of the letters in the formulas, but that can be included in another objective. If, in fact, the trainee is going to be using the characters in formulas, there is a need to be able to read them in upper and lower case, and perhaps in manuscript form. The objective can be valid, if the training includes reading the lists of characters in upper and lower case and in manuscript form, in alphabetic sequence, and in random sequence.

For practical reasons, criterion tests are samplings of the behavior representative of the objective statements. While the Greek alphabet example suggests that a more appropriate criterion test might have been used, it does represent a sampling of the behavior resulting from learning the Greek alphabet. This is where the evaluation program enters the picture. We use the criterion test to assess the progress of the trainee toward accomplishment of the training objectives, but we need another measure to assess the effectiveness of the *training* to meet the real needs of the job. The difference is important and should be remembered.

Another essential factor is time. Will the trainees retain the skill and knowledge after it is tested? Or, more importantly, will the trainee remember on the job? A comprehensive evaluation program will determine answers to these questions.

Using the Greek alphabet example, the training evaluation could ask the trainee, at the end of the course, to write a sampling of upper- and lower-case Greek letters, and several in script. The evaluation could request the trainee to repeat the test, or a variation of it, three months later when the trainee has had opportunity to use the skill and knowledge on the job. The measures, taken on all or a representative and random sampling of all trainees, will provide information about the effectiveness of the training in meeting the true course objectives. If the trainees are statistically capable of performing at the end of the training, but demonstrate skill deficiencies three months later on the job, it might be appropriate to examine the relevance of the objective to the job. If the skills learned in training are not used on the job, should they be part of the training? Or did the trainees simply not retain what they learned?

The previous paragraph suggests that the training can achieve the course objectives but still require revision to be more relevant to the job. Such is often the case, especially when we're dealing with new material. If a skill has not been trained before, or if the training technique is new, we should expect to make these kinds of errors. But even these errors will be fewer if the systematic approach is followed. The training developer must continually keep in mind that we're dealing with perhaps the most unpredictable creatures on earth—human beings. With all our research on the subject of human behavior, we still experience great difficulty in predicting reactions to specific situations. Plan on making substantial revisions throughout the life of any training program, especially the first few times it is used.

The evaluation task becomes even more difficult and complex when we need to assess a training program for managers to make better use of their time. First, there is an implicit assumption that the trainees are managers who use their time at a level that's less than desirable. Second, we assume that we can train managers to use their time wisely. This implies that there is a best way to manage one's time. Even if the subject is "impossible," the training developer may be convinced to undertake the program. The fact of the impossibility may not be apparent immediately, but may emerge during the development process. Whatever is done about the realization that a particular program may be impossible is subject to so many factors that we can't deal with them here. However, the end user or client for whom the program is being developed should be informed of your conclusions and the reasons that led to them.

Evaluation of a managers' time management training program may be extremely difficult, if not impossible, because we can establish few measures of the correct method. The correct method may be unknown or unprovable. We can only measure whether the trainee uses the skills and knowledge learned in the training. We can't establish, in a direct way, whether the managers' overall job performances are any better. But there are *indirect* methods of measurement that can be applied to this kind of situation. The evaluation program would use selected statistical techniques to assess the effectiveness of the program; the specific methodology is detailed later in this chapter.

Objectives can be evaluated, therefore, internal to the training and on the job. The two are different and both are important to an overall evaluation program.

**EVALUATION
DESIGN**

Training evaluation should be considered as an experiment and, therefore, should follow the standard practices and procedures employed in any experimental design. The rigor of the evaluation design will be reflected in the credibility of the data and results and, consequently, in its acceptance by others.

As in any other experiment, the design is completed *before* the evaluation is performed. That sounds like an obvious statement, but it's often not done, largely because evaluation is so often an afterthought. Evaluation design should really be part of the total training design.

The design begins with hypotheses based on each objective. The statistical design is established at the same time, as are the criteria for interpretation of the results of the statistical analysis.

With easy access to calculators and computers, even complex statistical operations are available in most training settings. Consequently, the calculation aspects of the design are of little consequence. It's much more important to select the proper statistical tools and data collection methods.

Using the example of the Greek alphabet training, let's explore some of the kinds of evaluation designs that could be used and the pros and cons of each.

Our first hypothesis is that the trainees are unable to recite the Greek alphabet when they begin the training. That hypothesis is necessary if we're going to establish the effectiveness of our training. If the trainees already can recite the Greek alphabet, our training is not only unnecessary, the evaluation of the results obtained by testing the trainees after training will provide misleading information.

A common approach to establish the skill or knowledge baseline is to administer a pre-training test to establish what the skill or knowledge level is prior to training. If the trainees have been selected according to the criteria established for the target population, none of them should be able to pass the pre-training test.

The second hypothesis states that, after the training, the trainees will be able to recite the Greek alphabet correctly in thirty seconds. A test administered after the training will provide the data necessary to determine if the objective was met. If the data reveal that none of the trainees could pass the test before training and all of them could pass it after training, then we can state unequivocally that the training was effective in bringing the trainees to the level where they could pass the criterion test. The only statistics required are percentages—zero percent passed the pre-training test, while 100 percent passed the post-training test.

Most of the time, the scores will not be 100 percent or zero. Another method for dealing with the data is to treat the differences that might be measurable. For example, in the pre-training test, performance might have been correct within sixty seconds by 90 percent of the trainees. The after-training performance could have been within thirty seconds by 80 percent of the group. How can we interpret these data? The data certainly suggest that the training had a positive result—the performance improved. Is the result significant? If we set our level of confidence at the .05 level or better, as we always should, we could run a t-test or a Pearson product-moment correlation to establish the significance level of the results. The particular statistic to be used is determined by the sample size and other factors, found in every statistics text. The point here is that statistics should be used and interpreted according to the rules established for them. They should be preselected and the criteria established before the first datum is collected.

When evaluating the results of the time management program, perhaps the measures could be based on the managers' performance reviews. Of course, those reviews are quite subjective in themselves and the managers selected might have been chosen because they already had high performance ratings. If that were the case, we couldn't expect the performance appraisals to reveal much—unless the performance declined after the training. That is always a possibility, especially if the managers' training proved to be inconsistent with the philosophy of the senior management who write the performance appraisals.

A meaningful measure of the effectiveness of the training in time management could be to measure the degree to which the trainees were applying the skills and knowledge acquired in the training. Data could be collected via interviews, questionnaires, and/or observation.

Another, long-term method for assessment of the results of the time management program could be to compare the achievements of the managers in the trained group with those peers who did not receive the training. If a statistically significant difference could be demonstrated, one could conclude that the time management training had a positive impact on the managers' careers.

Whatever the design, it should follow accepted experimental design procedures and be tempered with logical analysis.

Evaluation design should consider the following points at which the measurements are to be taken:

- Immediately after the learning.

- At the end of a lesson or module.

- At the end of the course.

- Shortly after beginning to use the skills and knowledge on the job.

- Three to six months after completing training.

- One to three years after training.

- Five to ten years after training.

The decision to use any of the above is made on the basis of the earlier hypotheses. The list is included here as a reminder that training evaluation may continue for many years and have a substantial impact on the total design of a program. The list could be applied in a management training program where every manager in the organization is required to complete the training. The short-term and long-term evaluations provide information about the value of the training and the behavior of the people trained. The information also provides data for use in revising the basic program.

An ongoing evaluation program requires careful and thorough planning, but the rewards can be well worth the effort and relatively small costs associated with the data collection, analysis, and reporting.

EVALUATION METHODS

Evaluation of training seems to have as many variations as practitioners. Methods, approaches, and philosophies differ, according to the individual responsible for the evaluation program and according to the needs of the organization.

For example, a large organization felt that a two-hour new employee orientation program would not only help the new employees become productive sooner, but it would reduce the numbers of inquiries about benefits to the personnel department. Management wanted to know if the new employees felt that the orientation addressed their concerns and made them feel better, in general, about the company. They also wanted to know if there was a reduction in the numbers of inquiries to Personnel by new employees.

Many methods could be used to gather the data and evaluate the program, but management imposed a restriction—to perform the evaluation at minimum cost. Cost is a factor that is almost always present and must be considered as much as the design itself. The impact of cost on design can often be more substantial than any other single factor. Cost constraints, if viewed as opportunities for creativity rather than as problems, can lead to innovative and elegant solutions to otherwise mundane problems.

In this case, the solution was easy. One of the objectives of the orientation was to reduce the numbers of calls to Personnel. A corollary of that objective is that the new employees were to acquire sufficient information so that they wouldn't feel compelled to call as often as their predecessors had. The evaluator went one step further, assuming that if there were no negative reactions to the orientation, the new employees were satisfied with it. Armed with those elements, the evaluation was based on the numbers of calls after the orientation compared to new employees' calls before the orientation was instituted. Fortunately, the personnel department maintained records of this type to justify their staffing levels. The evaluator was quite pleased at having designed an evaluation scheme that required no new data collection and was accomplished at the lowest possible cost. Management also was pleased with the approach.

That kind of evaluation is simple and inexpensive only when it is planned. Meaningful evaluations don't just happen. It's difficult enough to demonstrate cause and effect when dealing with training and the associated evaluation, but it becomes more difficult to establish credibility for an evaluation when the relationships are established after the fact.

In the case of the orientation program, improvement in the call rate could have been a function of many other factors, such as a more informed group of new employees, different economic conditions, change in the new hire policies, etc. This is a good example of a successful evaluation that could have become an unsuccessful one if the evaluator had stated that the orientation program reduced the numbers of calls by new hires to Personnel by X percent. That statement is one that assumes more than the data had demonstrated. A more correct statement would have been that the numbers of calls by new hires to the personnel department was reduced from an average of 8.4 to 3.6 during the first six months of employment *after* the new employee orientation was introduced.

The latter statement does not imply cause and effect, while the first one does. The second statement described what happened, without attributing a reason. The reasons, if considered important, are the subject of a different kind of evaluation.

Our evaluator carried the assessment still further to provide management with the information it was seeking. The real question that concerned management was whether the cost of the training and the associated time off the job by the new employees saved at least the equivalent in time in the personnel department. The evaluator was able to obtain the cost figures for the orientation program development for each new employee, as well as the average cost of a phone call to Personnel. The results were clear—the program cost far more than was saved in Personnel. But the orientation program was already developed and required minimal maintenance. The evaluator now subtracted the development cost from the calculations and found that the costs, while still higher for the orientation than for the calls to Personnel, were much closer. Management concluded that the costs were justified, since there were fewer disruptions in the personnel department and the new employees were able to spend more productive time on the job. Those were factors the evaluator didn't even consider, but if the evaluator had presented those elements, without the supporting data, they might easily have been rejected because they made assumptions that were beyond the scope of the training evaluation and of the data.

The inter-organizational relationships maintained by the evaluator can influence the acceptability of the data and of the reports and recommendations made by the evaluator. It's far better to be cautious when making statements about a program based on experimental or observational data. *It's essential, if credibility of the evaluation process is to be established and maintained, that interpretation of results does not go beyond what the data demonstrate.*

Data Collection

Besides the different methods used for establishing the evaluation to be performed, there are a number of ways to implement the data collection. The kind of data collection often determines the quality of the data and the credibility of the results and recommendations based on that data. For example, there is a marked difference between collecting data based on opinion or belief, and observation of performance. In other words, you can ask a group of trainees if they can perform the task that was just presented, or ask them to perform the task individually. It's clear that the former approach, while it might shed some light on the trainees' attitudes and perceptions, is not nearly as meaningful as having an expert observe performance of the newly learned activities. The fact that the observer is expert is equally important, unless the criteria are provided or the task performance is so self-evident that a nonexpert observer can distinguish correct from incorrect performance.

The ideal method for collecting data during a training program is to build the data collection into the training as an integral part. Exercises and tests that are used in the training are appropriate for the evaluation of the training. As with other parts of the training evaluation, the embedded evaluation should be planned and criteria established for use of the data before the program is first used. Adjustments are often appropriate, based on the initial program presentations.

Data collected during the training program are used to evaluate the degree to which the training meets its objectives. It is useful for assessing the trainees' reactions and acceptance of the program, and for determining the reactions of the instructors regarding the usability of the materials, the amount of time consumed compared to the estimates of the developer, and other information pertaining to the trainees or to the program itself.

The data collected during the training may come from several sources, principally the trainees, the instructors, or from "outside" observers. When trainees or instructors are asked to participate in an evaluation program, they may be on guard for fear that they will be evaluated unfairly or they may react negatively to being evaluated at all. If, however, the "normal" classroom activities also provide data for evaluation, there is less disruption and apprehension.

Introduction of an "outside" observer into the classroom is often accepted, but viewed by both the trainees and the instructors as disruptive and threatening. The use of recording devices and one-way screens are also viewed negatively, as being surreptitious. If there are no other reasonable methods for collecting essential data, then the outsider may be necessary. If outsiders are used, their presence should be explained and they should be as unobtrusive as possible. There should be no special acknowledgment when an observer enters the classroom. The observer's presence should be routine. Clipboards and stopwatches present generally negative images and should be avoided, as should notetaking or recording. The evaluation design should be established so that the observer acquires information that can't be obtained directly from the embedded evaluation tools.

Data collected after completion of the training most often is obtained from the trainees and their managers, directly or indirectly. Direct methods are interviews and questionnaires, while indirect methods are performance appraisals, promotion lists and announcements, news releases, and other pre-established indicators.

Some of the sources are not always available, so alternatives must be sought. If the evaluation is for sales personnel, it's easy, in most organizations, to obtain sales figures in dollar amounts and numbers of sales. If the evaluation is for repair of engines, other on-the-job measures can usually be made, such as productivity, return rate, and average difficulty level of all jobs. Experts in every job can identify the criteria for job success.

**REPORTING
EVALUATION
RESULTS**

Evaluation reports should be prepared using a format that's consistent from one report to the next. The content of the report should include a factual statement first, perhaps in the form of a fact sheet, including:

- Name of the training program.

- Subject or topic of the training.

- Level or class of training.

- Target population.

- Training methods used.

- Dates of training.

- Location of training.

- Type of training (classroom, self-instructional, etc.).

- Number of trainees.

- Number of instructors.

- Course duration.

- Amount of time per training day in session.

- Kinds of measures taken.

- Results of measures taken.

- Evaluation score (against pre-specified criteria).

The fact sheet contains "hard" data, which is defined as that which requires no interpretation. It's a clear statement of *what* happened, without explaining why. The fact sheet can, in many cases, fit onto a single page and it provides the information essential in an evaluation. The remainder of the evaluation report is usually quite lengthy, attempting to explain *why* the results were obtained. Experience has demonstrated that the more divergent the results are from those predicted, the longer the report.

The actual evaluation data are generally of no interest to most people, but they should be included in an appendix to the report, unless it's too voluminous to be practical. In that event, they should be placed in a library or other file to which others may have access. However the data are stored, they should be retrievable, since additional studies may be performed later.

If data are on punched cards, they should be stored on more convenient media and retained for a minimum of five years, unless the data won't be required again.

Why should an evaluation report explain why the results were achieved? Isn't it enough to know that the training succeeded or failed?

There are many reasons why a training program succeeds or fails but, more to the point, often there isn't a clear indication that it passed or failed. That doubt is largely in the minds of the evaluators, since the statistics indicate significance or no significance. A level of confidence at .07 is not statistically significant, even though it's closer to significance than .22. The real difficulty occurs when there are some variables in the evaluation that prove to be statistically significant, while others are not.

This is where interpretation and judgment are required. The evaluator should remember that the purpose of the evaluation is to determine if the training meets its goals and objectives and to identify the weak points in the training so they may be strengthened.

Excuses and alibis have no place in an evaluation report. Reasons are not the same as excuses and alibis, although sometimes the differences are not apparent. An excuse or alibi is defined as speculation that there is a cause-and-effect relationship between the variable and the performance. A reason is where there is evidence of cause and effect. For example, if a cold epidemic during the training affected half the class, using that as a cause for not meeting the criteria is an *excuse*. On the other hand, if research data demonstrate a performance deficit of a specific percentage can be expected when trainees have colds, then that is a *reason*.

The training developers are interested to learn how to improve the training. The evaluation report should describe in detail what the performance of the trainees was like on those elements where objectives have not been met.

Training evaluation has not been overwhelmingly successful, for a number of reasons. First, not too many training developers seek criticism and public assessment of their work. Second, the cost of the evaluation may be more than the sponsor of the evaluation is willing to pay, especially if the evaluation is labor-intensive, as most are when they're not embedded in the training. The third, and perhaps the saddest reason why training evaluation is not done more, is that the people paying the bills aren't convinced of the validity of the evaluations that have been done or that they believe can be done.

If an independent agency pays for the evaluation, there tends to be an aura of "inspection." If the agent sponsoring the training supports the evaluation, there is a suspicion that there is a vested interest in the results, whether positive or negative. These reasons are arguments for embedded evaluation. Out of fairness to all concerned, the evaluation should be an integral part of the training program so that it becomes immaterial who performs the data analysis and reporting, so long as they are competent professionals.

22

Alternatives to Training

Workers in the training field hear the cry from management, "If they can't do the job, let's train them." Training is the quick answer for performance problems, but it's not always the only, nor even the best answer.

Let's make an assumption, since we really have no proof, that a *perfect* system requires no special training, because the operation is obvious, rational, and self-guiding. In other words, if everything worked the way a self-service elevator operates, trainers could be out of work. But even self-service elevator design makes some assumptions about the people who use elevators. Elevator designers assume that the people using elevators know that they go up and down to specific floors if the proper buttons are pressed. A person who had never seen an elevator before, or who didn't know the purpose of the elevator, might not find the contraption of perfect design. But even that individual could determine those facts by simple observation or, at most, a single ride on an elevator. The point is that if we can design the object activity, system, or machine so that its uses and functions are obvious, training requirements can be reduced or eliminated completely.

IMPROVING SYSTEM DESIGN

Obviously, there are many perfect systems already in our everyday lives. If we see a pencil or a screwdriver, or a teacup, we automatically know how to perform basic tasks using them. What we may not know automatically is how to use them to perform secondary activities. Anyone, without training, can make a mark with a pencil, but how many people can write their names without some training?

Much of the training performed today is necessary because the subjects of the training were not perfectly designed. Perfect design is sometimes physically impossible, while in other instances, it's simply too expensive. It is sometimes cheaper to train people to use the system rather than spend the extra money necessary to eliminate the need for training. The decision to design a less-than-perfect system should be a conscious one, and not left to chance or happen by default. Sometimes the training costs far exceed the costs that might be incurred to make the system more perfect.

Of course, many systems cannot be perfected because some skills must be practiced for proficiency. Even though we may invent the most perfect scalpel possible, performance of surgical procedures requires training, even though the act of cutting with a scalpel, in the generic sense, requires no training. In this example, the scalpel may be a perfectly designed instrument, but its applications are not. If the human body were marked, "make a 13mm. incision here 8mm. deep to remove appendix," even that wouldn't be sufficient, since the bodies would necessarily have to be designed identically or the messages printed on them would need to change as the body grew and weight changed. Besides, the appendix would need to be labeled somehow, including instructions to complete the procedure once it was found. This example borders on the ridiculous, but illustrates the concept of perfect design and the frequent impossibility of achieving it.

In a more realistic vein, think about how well designed a public pay telephone is, from a user's point of view. If the user is able to read, the instructions for using the instrument are printed at eye level, the coin slots are easy to find, and the dial is easy to read and to use. The dial tone is audible to persons with normal hearing, and the busy signal and ring are easily recognized. There is even a "last resort" method for obtaining assistance from an operator. The system is well designed, but how many people know or can figure out what the lower left and lower right keys are that have appeared on telephones during the past few years? How are we going to learn to use those keys? Is the telephone company going to train us, or are they going to continue to devise near-perfect systems? The choice will be made consciously, and we're betting that the use of those new keys will require virtually no special training. When the time comes, their use will be obvious.

Many of the new personal and business computer systems incorporate what are called in the trade "user friendly" qualities. To the provider of the system, that means a person who is not a computer programmer can use the system. To the average user, it means that the system may be approached with less trepidation than otherwise might be the case. To a trainer, it means that little or no training should be required because the system will be self-explanatory and replete with menus, prompts, and "help" messages.[1]

Training, while often the most immediately thought of solution to performance problems, is not always the only or the best approach. In the sections that follow, we'll review some of the types of alternatives to training and the kinds of conditions where you can expect to find them.

There is a marked difference between treating symptoms and treating the *causes* of performance problems. Taking aspirin for a migraine headache, for example, won't remove the cause for a migraine headache, but it might remove the painful symptoms. Treating symptoms where the cause is unknown or untreatable is useful and efficacious, but it is temporary and requires repetition, sometimes with high frequency. Removal of the cause of the problem, if done properly and completely, removes the symptoms permanently. A toothache may result from an abscess and may be ameliorated by a painkiller, but removal of the abscess will remove the cause of the pain.

We tend to develop stock responses to situations or conditions. For example, we take aspirin for pain. We know that headaches can have many causes, and don't really care about the cause of an occasional headache. If the headaches persist in frequency or severity, we become concerned and, while we may continue to take our painkillers, we seek professional help to find out *why* we're having those severe headaches.

Headaches can have many causes, and our physician may order numerous diagnostic tests to determine why the headaches exist so that the cause may be treated or removed. Sounds simple, doesn't it? However, diagnosis is often much more difficult than the treatment, in training as well as in other fields.

TRAINING TO TREAT SYMPTOMS

A Case Example

Let's examine a case of human performance on the job. A large company was engaged in the manufacture of electronic printed circuit

---

[1] A *menu* is a list of choices the user can make. A *prompt* is an indication by the computer that the user can or should do something at a certain place. A *"help"* message is a computer response to a user request for additional information.

boards used in a large proportion of the company's products. These boards were not only complex and expensive, but there was no other source for them. A separate plant was established for their manufacture. The most modern equipment was installed and the company paid the best wages to acquire the best available people to produce these critical components.

The plant included a receiving and warehousing section, where the primary components were received, counted, tested, stored, and distributed to the production department. A special section prepared kits that were used by the automated equipment that mechanically inserted a large number of the components into the circuit boards. The unfinished boards were then taken to an assembly line where rows of workers at workbenches inserted other components by hand, following a drawing. Each worker inserted up to five components and passed the board to the next station, where more components were added. The board was passed through about six stations in that manner, until all the components were installed on the board. The last station in this part of the process was an inspector, who checked the boards against a master drawing. Rejects were placed in a separate bin for later rework. The reject rate was extremely low.

The boards were then moved, via conveyor, to a soldering section. Here the boards traveled through an automatic soldering process. They entered a large enclosed machine at one end and came out the other end with every connection securely soldered. As the boards exited the machine, they were cleaned and stacked in racks, ready for a process called burn-in. The boards were placed in the burn-in ovens for up to forty-eight hours, where they were heat stressed to bring component failures to the surface. This process reduced the field failure rate of the boards.

The final step in the production of the boards was testing. Complex circuit boards can only be tested, economically, using sophisticated computer testers. These testers, while expensive, identify only some of the gross failures of the boards, without pinpointing the precise component that is the cause of the less than adequate performance of the board. Consequently, the test personnel were required to be highly skilled electronic technicians to be able to diagnose the many nonroutine faults that appeared on the boards. The numbers of test machines were finite, and the numbers of skilled technicians were never sufficient. The testing section operated on a three-shift, seven-day per week schedule and still was unable to keep up with the production schedule. The reject rate at the test stage was never below 30 percent. The industry standard was closer to 10 percent.

To make matters even worse, the boards were repaired by a large rework section. The rework consisted of desoldering and resoldering components identified as defective by the test section. These boards also had to be reprocessed through the test section after they were repaired, thereby increasing the workload on the already overtaxed section.

The plant manager observed that all sections were meeting their productivity goals, with the glaring exception of the test section. Higher management was beginning to apply pressure on the plant manager to improve performance. There was a real threat that the plant manager's job was in jeopardy. The company considered efficient operation of this plant to be critical to the production of their primary products.

The plant manager concluded that the test technicians required more training so they could work faster and better and get the backlog cleared. He called in a team of training experts to determine precisely what the best training might be for those people. What the plant manager really wanted to know was which of the available electronics training programs available on the market would be best suited to these particular technicians.

The training consultants proceeded with their investigation, to define the training requirements. After meeting with the plant management team, they met with the test technicians and soon concluded that there might have been more than met the eye in this situation. The test technicians had their own ideas, based on experience and their training. The test technicians seemed, by and large, well trained and qualified for the job. There appeared to be simply too much work to be processed with the physical resources available. One of the factors that helped convince the trainers that they might have been dealing with a symptom in the test section was the fact that the experienced, senior technicians were able to perform all the necessary work and were helpful to the less experienced people.

If the testing backlog was truly a symptom, what was the cause? Observation and discussions with workers throughout the plant, plus a little logic, led the trainers to the conclusion that the primary cause of the high error rates was the fact that the workers who inserted the components manually were making many errors that were not caught by the inspectors at the ends of their lines. The workers received little or no feedback about their errors, so they continued to repeat them, thereby being the major contributor to the high backlog in the testing section. Secondary causes of the problem were numerous, but the key appeared to be the simplest operation in the entire plant.

The differences in the potential results and associated costs between treating the symptom or removing the cause in this case were enormous. Unfortunately, the plant manager refused to accept the findings of the training team, insisting that all that was required was training of the technicians. The plant manager was subsequently replaced by another manager, who also refused to accept the recommendations. The problem persists, years later.

Sometimes, as we have seen in this example, finding the cause is not sufficient to solve the problem. On the other hand, what would have been gained if the trainers had gone along with the plant manager and prescribed a training program for the test technicians? At worst, the plant manager could have a scapegoat to point a finger at—experts who were unable to solve the problem. We see that the trainer should understand the situation in as broad a scope as possible to understand whether symptoms or causes are being treated. Treating symptoms that will improve performance is better than doing nothing, even if we know the cause and that its removal would provide more improvement.

How could we tell if the test technicians required training or if the performance problem lay somewhere else?

The answer is that we compare the way the operation is supposed to operate with the way it operates, and then we observe the operation and ask questions.

Even that statement sounds simple. How is a training specialist supposed to know how the factory is supposed to operate? Again, the answer is simple—ask the people who do know. Then, it's a matter of comparing what should be to what is.

We need to consider three essential elements of the operation:

- Job definition.

- Organization structure.

- Operational procedures.

Let's look at each of those elements separately.

Job definition includes the activities necessary for successful job performance; the skills and knowledge necessary to be qualified for the job. It includes the inputs to the job, the actions performed, and the output from the activity.

Organizational structure includes consideration of *where* the inputs to the job originate and *where* they are sent. It also includes definition of the supervisory and oversight relationships, including inspection, timekeeping, safety, and other administrative and management functions that impinge on the job. An organizational chart may be useful to show the work relationships.

Operational procedures incorporate the frequency and quantity of input, process, and output, as well as the standards for the work. Standards include production rates and product quality, as they apply to the job. Operational procedures illustrate the job activities and the flow of work through the job. A functional flow diagram is useful to depict the operational procedures.

In actual practice, collection of the three kinds of data defined above will give the training developer a basic understanding of the job and the system in which it may be embedded. It may highlight relationships, potential bottlenecks, and problem areas.

When collection of the relevant data has been completed and the information organized, review the results of the data collection with a person who is not only knowledgeable in the operation, but who is currently functioning in that organization. Moreover, it's useful if that person is an incumbent of the job in question. Verification should be taken one step further—to the management of the function.

This verification step often uncovers some of the basic problems leading to performance deficiencies. When discussing the job with the incumbent, the job holder's emphasis may be to do the best quality work possible, while the management states the goal is as many units as possible. If management emphasizes quantity while the workers stress quality, there is not only a failure of communication, but there is a reason why management's expectations will probably not be met. Training won't resolve those differences, but performance can be improved by looking for ways to reconcile the differences and by changing the job definition, the organization, or procedures.

The approach is applicable to any kind of job, on a production line, in sales, maintenance, management, or in the professions. The essential elements are defining what is expected, comparing that to what actually happens, and identifying the differences. Once we determine *why* the differences exist, we can establish whether training is a solution to the performance problems, or whether an alternative to training might be more effective.

Sometimes it costs less to train than to implement any alternative to training, assuming that training will remedy the performance problem. Regardless of how we might feel, as trainers, costs are almost always the determining factor in decisions regarding training or alternatives to training. Costs are measured, not only in dollars, but in time, labor, materials, and productivity loss that may occur between the time of decision and the time of implementation.

Costs are a factor in all applications—in a school system, in the government, in the military, in industry. They are more critical in some areas than in others, but the training developer should always be tuned in to them, especially when considering whether to recommend training or an alternative. If we design solutions that cost more than the problem, our solution probably will never be implemented, and our credibility will be damaged.

Most often, the costs for the alternatives to training will be less, especially when large numbers of people are to be trained over a long period of time. The factors that loom largest when considering costs for a training program are the numbers of trainee hours represented by the program. In large training programs, *minutes* of training time are examined carefully, asking:

- Is this task or activity necessary for job performance?

- Can the learning be accomplished in less time?

- Are the performance criteria too high?

- Can the skills and knowledge be acquired in another way?

In recent years, a remarkable number of trainee hours and millions of dollars have been saved by determining that parts of an ongoing training program were not necessary. Sometimes the alternative to training was *no training* because the skill or knowledge was determined to be superfluous or nonessential to the job. In other cases, the training was eliminated in favor of job aids, extended apprenticeship, or personnel changes.

Training programs that continue to survive are generally those that are maintained to reflect the current needs of the trainees and the jobs. The jobs and their requirements change over time, and each change should be examined to determine if the required skills and knowledge can be acquired by the trainees in a faster, better, or less expensive way.

Cost considerations may sound like someone else's problem to a training developer, but training programs require sponsors whose money is being spent. Those sponsors expect to receive value for their money and are favorably impressed by training developers who understand the economic elements of training development and program maintenance. To a sponsor, less is best—the ideal is the mininum amount of training for the trainee to acquire a level of competence sufficient to perform the job essentials.

The other side of the coin is that the sponsor may be unwilling to invest even the minimum required to meet that basic objective of job competence. When sponsor frugality mitigates against adequate training, it's time to educate the sponsor. Failing that, the training developer is wise to withdraw from the battle. Inadequate training is frequently worse than none at all, since trainees are expected to perform after training, regardless of its quality, while the untrained are excused from such expectations. Of course, the implications are different if we're talking about training infantry, salespeople, or preschoolers, but the principles apply to all.

and should be prepared to assess selection criteria at any time. As trainers, perhaps we can help educate the managers to the implications in cost and productivity to the organization of a valid personnel acquisition program.

As with personnel selection, some training goals and objectives become sacred cows that can't be touched or challenged because of tradition, bias, or conviction. A classic example of a large organization's assessment of a set of objectives is when a public utility demonstrated that it was unnecessary to train telephone repair people in electricity and electrical theory. This part of the comprehensive program required about six weeks and cost millions of dollars per year. The examination of the job against its requirements forced the management of this huge organization to reconsider a "fact" that they had accepted for their entire careers. The alternative to the electricity training was no training in electricity and earlier graduation to the job.

Similarly, the United States Navy, under severe budget pressure, scrutinized its training programs to save *minutes* in each one. The effort had a large payoff. Useless segments were discovered and removed from the programs. The need to assess objectives against the job is an ongoing one, and offers a potentially valuable alternative to training.

The examples cited above required comparison of the facts with credible data, collected in a rigorous, scientific manner. Argument alone is not sufficiently convincing, especially when the subject being considered is one close to the hearts of senior management.

A job aid is any device that helps a person perform the job. A job aid may be a memory jogger, reference card, template, gauge, etc. If a rock carried in the hand of army recruits reminds them which is the left and which is the right hand, the rock is a job aid. So are the flight simulators used by pilots and astronauts.

Job aids take many forms. Some are exotic and expensive, while others are common, simple, and inexpensive. Tools are job aids, in the generic sense. The make the job easier and, in some cases, they make the job possible.

Job aids can be very effective alternatives to training and a training developer should be constantly on the alert for the application of job aids to replace segments of training. For example, if speed is determined not to be a factor, a reference list could be provided to the trainee so that items could be looked up rather than be memorized. As the trainee becomes more familiar with the job, the aid may become less necessary.

An effective job aid is one that begins as a *training aid* to help the trainee with the initial learning, and then is taken onto the job to be used as a job aid until no longer required.

Some of the best job aids may be designed by the trainees as they're learning. Complex procedures, for example, may be painstakingly presented in the training materials. The presentation may be sufficient for the trainee to perform the activity correctly, but not to remember the details. Having performed the tasks once, the trainee might devise a simplified guide to the operation that enhances total performance.

Training developers should be alert to trainee-developed job aids, since they can be used to develop aids that can be distributed to future trainees, and may reduce the total required training time for the program.

23

Writing Styles

Writing style has become more important in recent years, with the increase in self-administered training and computer-assisted instruction. More written material is probably used by learners today than ever before. This is especially evident in institutions outside the school and university systems. Business and industry, the government, military, and the professions are all using more and more self-study and self-administered training programs.

These programs are usually designed to make it as easy as possible for the trainee to learn and to acquire new skills. The language and writing style are important to the trainees, even though they may not be aware of either.

Aside from preparing written materials at the reading level of the target populations, it's equally important to present a style that is nonthreatening, yet authoritative; friendly, yet insightful and proper. There's no need to be formal and stuffy. We want people to read the materials and to learn from them. We don't want the materials themselves to get in the way of our objectives. We want the trainees to learn the material and to meet the program's objectives.

Let's look at some of the style considerations that influence learner reactions.

Formal style is represented by proper language use, with little or no relaxing of the rules of language or of conduct. In a formal style, the writer doesn't usually reach out and touch the reader, but maintains a proper distance. Formal style tends to be somewhat stilted and risks stuffiness in its precision and correctness. Contractions are not used, nor are slang expressions and pronouns.

The formal style is appropriate when we are trying to impress other people, especially subordinates. Formal language is found in orientation programs, for example, where we want it to be clearly understood that we mean business.

That's not to say the informal style's for foolin' around. The informal style generally takes a conventional tone and makes trainees feel more comfortable. It takes the trainees by the hand and offers to explore together the wonders of the subject.

Both formal and informal styles have their places. Care is necessary to avoid being overbearing in the formal style or condescending or patronizing in the informal. These are dangers that can be avoided by conscious effort and by careful review and editing before trying it with trainees.

While consistency of writing style may be considered desirable, shifting from informal to formal can create an impression that the material has suddenly become more important. That effect can be used to advantage by the training developer. By the same token, a shift from a formal style in a particularly difficult segment of the training might be followed by a more relaxed, informal style while the trainee has time to regroup and assimilate the material.

So long as informal is not interpreted as sloppy or careless, it's quite acceptable and should be used as the trainer considers appropriate. However, there is no excuse for training developers to use improper grammar, spelling, or punctuation. Errors detract from the credibility of the materials and every reasonable step should be taken to avoid them. A good editor can be a training developer's best friend, especially when the materials are to be self-administered.

This subject carries with it a great deal of emotional bias, and discussions about jargon can lead to heated debate, if not violence. So let's get it out on the table—*jargon represents an attempt to restrict communication and understanding* to a select group who are "in" on the special meanings of the argot. In many instances, jargon becomes a protective device that ensures the survival and indispensability of a group.

Whenever a group of people spends a great deal of time together, working in the same arena, they develop their own shorthand language to make communication easier. So they say. Jargon may use fewer syllables and letters than the words they replace, but they tend to become elitist symbols and a kind of statement that says, "Nyah, nyah, we know something you don't."

Similarly, acronyms and other letter-oriented language tend to keep outsiders from understanding, often making a lesson appear more difficult and complex than it really is.

A legitimate language does develop in virtually every special area of human activity whether it's a scientific discipline or a game. This language is not jargon, but a necessary adjunct to the everyday language everyone knows. A carburetor, for instance, has no other universally recognized word in the English language. To be sure, there are slang words for it and there is also jargon associated with the device and its functions.

The goal of training materials is to communicate. Jargon and alphabet soup restrict communication and should be avoided in training programs. Unless there are truly mitigating circumstances, training programs should *not* include jargon. It interferes with the mainstream learning activities when the trainee needs to learn a new, unnecessary language.

A good test of training materials is to read through the entire set and mark each word and abbreviation whose meaning is different from that of the standard dictionary. If there are few or none, the training materials will probably be better than if there are many. If any of those items are used, they should be included in a glossary. If there are none, there is no need for a glossary. There is only a small glossary in this book because a conscious effort was made to exclude jargon and special technical terms.

A generally accepted convention for using abbreviations is to spell out the term the first time it's used and include the abbreviation in parentheses immediately following the initial use. If the writer considers the abbreviation one that will not be easily recalled, or if the second use is far into the document, then the same presentation can be repeated one or two more times.

AVOIDING SEXIST LANGUAGE

The only times that the use of masculine and feminine pronouns should be used are when the training is directed toward an exclusive group of one or the other. These days, jobs no longer have gender, and the only application might be if we're training mothers or fathers. If we're training both, together, the appropriate pronoun is "they" and the nouns are "parent" and "spouse."

Because we don't know in advance if the trainees will be male or female or a mixed group, trainers must avoid the use of masculine and feminine pronouns in the training materials. It's much easier to avoid using gendered words than it is to change them. Ways to avert disaster in this sphere are to:

- Use plurals so "they" becomes the appropriate pronoun.

- Avoid the combined he/she and hers/his.

- Refrain from making up new words, such as "person-hole cover" or "peoplekind."

- Assume the gender of the individual being discussed only when it's necessary to make the point.

- Avoid nouns suggesting gender, such as actress, schoolmarm, maid, policeman, fireman, salesman, lineman.

- When using people's names, unless the gender is important for some reason, use names that could be male or female, such as Pat, Ronnie, or Lynn, or use initials, such as J.B.

- Avoid casting people of either sex in stereotyped roles, such as female telephone operators, nurses, and secretaries; and male soldiers, engineers, and technicians.

Materials that include arbitrary reference to gender are dated and lose credibility with trainees of both sexes.

There are still arguments over whether "chairman" should now be "chairperson," "chair," or simply "president." Training developers have the option of choosing the words that, in their judgment, best fit the situation. It isn't necessary for everyone to agree. The issue is important here only if it affects learning. If the trainees become upset by a choice of words, they'll be distracted and the learning will probably suffer. If that occurs, the offending word should be replaced with an inoffensive one.

Illustrations should follow the same guidelines. Use neutered figures, if figures must be used, where the gender of the individual is not important to the message.

In the training materials, avoid statments such as, "Ask your instructor if he/she has. . . ." Use instead, "Ask your instructor for. . . ."

Use of the pronoun *you* can keep the writer out of difficulty with respect to the neutered phrases. For example, "If you do this, then you won't have to . . ." is different from "If Jan does this, then he/she won't have to. . . ."

This writer has found that, at least in the beginning, it's a good practice to develop an image of the audience for whom the materials are being prepared. That audience is comprised of an equal number of male and female trainees, with a proportional sprinkling of other groups representative of the total population. By retaining this kind of mental image, it becomes easier to address the people correctly. Practice makes the task still easier.

Overwriting can be deadly in a training program, especially in self-administered materials, where the trainees are working on their own. Dense text has an overpowering effect—it intimidates people and they develop a negative attitude toward the training when they first open a wordy or weighty tome.

White space exists not only physically on the printed page, it also has psychological impact when the materials impress the trainee as being light and airy, as opposed to being heavy and cumbersome. Even the color of the book's cover can have that kind of impact. A white binder, for example, is viewed more positively than a dull gray one. If the white binder is pleasingly printed in bright colors, so much the better.

These characteristics speak to the trainees, telling them, "See, I'm not so bad. Don't be afraid of me."

Cartoons and other line drawings have similar effects on trainees, creating a positive feeling and a willingness to get into the materials and to learn.

White space is often created in trainee's materials by leaving blank areas in which the learners are asked to write or draw. This kind of white space is effective in producing the desired openness in the materials but, more importantly, it converts the materials into a more useful workbook and potential reference for use on the job. Of course, when trainees write in the materials, they are no longer usable by others. Whether reuse is a factor should be determined in each instance.

Of course, wide variations exist in the kinds of presentations that appeal to different people. There is no universally appealing quality or formula for sure success. Knowledge of the tastes and idiosyncrasies of the target population are most useful when considering matters of eye appeal and acceptability.

Generally applicable guidelines that ordinarily increase the eye appeal of textual materials are:

- Use space-and-a-half or double spacing, except when quoting or setting off special short segments. Avoid single spacing whenever possible.

- Use wide margins all around.

- Use short paragraphs, with an extra space between.

- Use underlining and boldfacing judiciously—it's easy to overdo, thereby losing some of the desired impact.

- Consider using boldface headings and marginal notations for ready reference by the trainees.

- Consider use of colored papers and colored inks for the materials, with different colored pages coded for some specific purpose.

- Use block format. It's easier to pick up the lead word in a segment.

- Use illustrations and photos freely, but be sure photographs are of high contrast and not too cluttered.

- Avoid being overly "creative" with layouts, colors, or other devices that might be distracting.

- Seek professional help to ensure artistic and esthetic qualities.

While, as a professional, you might be more concerned with the content of your materials, other people do judge books by their covers—and their general appearance. The cosmetics, while perhaps not essential to your message, may be critical to the kind of acceptance you want your materials to have. If you don't feel comfortable with this aspect of training development, professional assistance can be well worth the time and costs.

If you select, rather than produce illustrations and photographs, don't violate any copyrights that may exist.

BINDING AND PACKAGING

The most common form of binding for training materials used outside of school systems is loose-leaf binders, which are used because they offer the greatest flexibility and the lowest cost. Both instructors and trainees can add pages to a loose-leaf binder. Loose-leaf bindings also make it easier to produce photocopies of forms and other materials that may be required for use in the training.

Even if loose-leaf binders are used, the materials may still be printed professionally and the covers and contents can have the appearance of quality and professionalism. A quality appearance can be achieved by printing on both sides, on sixty pound paper of good grade. While some photocopy machines produce excellent copy quality, the appearance of quality is generally enhanced if the pages are produced by an offset process. Actually, if sufficient numbers are to be produced, offset becomes less expensive than photocopy.

While the packaging attention is most focused on the trainee's materials, presentation of the instructor's materials can be important also, especially if the instructors had little or nothing to do with the development of the program. Instructors prefer to be considered as important as the trainees and enjoy using materials that are packaged attractively.

Packaging materials should be attractive and tasteful, the effect being to present a nonthreatening and pleasant introduction. The program will stand on its own merits.

Epilogue

If this book has helped you do even a small part of your job, it has achieved its major objective. As you use the process, it will become easier and, in time, many of the steps you followed may be done mentally. As you become surer of the path, the journey becomes easier.

Good Luck!

Selected References

Following is a short list of selected further readings, chosen for their coverage of the subject for students or practitioners who desire to broaden themselves in areas broached by this book. Some of these materials elaborate the views of author, while others may be in conflict in certain instances. For the person who wants to delve into research in instructional psychology, the Resnick reference is recommended. Most of the listed references include additional bibliographies to urge readers on to a greater depth of understanding of this complex and often controversial subject.

Anderson, R. H. *Selecting and Developing Media for Instruction.* New York: Van Nostrand Reinhold, 1976.

Craig, R. L. *Training & Development Handbook* (2nd Ed.). New York: McGraw-Hill, 1979.

Gardner, J. E. *Training Interventions in Job Skills Development.* Reading MA: Addison-Wesley, 1981.

Mager, R. F. *Preparing Instructional Objectives* (2nd Ed.). Belmont CA: Fearon Publishers, 1975.

Mager, R. F., & Pipe, P. *Analyzing Performance Problems.* Belmont CA: Fearon Publishers, 1973.

Miller, V. A. *The Guidebook for International Trainers in Business and Industry.* New York: Van Nostrand Reinhold, 1979.

NAVEDTRA 106A. *Interservice Procedures for Instructional Systems Development: Executive Summary and Model.* Philadelphia: Naval Publications and Forms Center, 1975.

NAVEDTRA 110A. *Procedures for Instructional Systems Development.* Philadelphia: Naval Publications and Forms Center, 1981.

O'Neil, H. F. (Ed.). *Computer-Based Instruction, A State-of-the-Art Assessment.* New York: Academic Press, 1981.

Resnick, L. B. Instructional Psychology. In M. P. Rosenzweig & L. W. Porter (Eds.), *Annual Review of Psychology,* 1981, *32,* 659–704.

Glossary

ACRONYM. A word made from the initial letters of other words. Usually acronyms are capitalized, but sometimes the acronyms become accepted words and are written as any other word, such as radar or snafu, which originally were acronyms.

AUTHOR LANGUAGES. Refer to applications of computer assisted instruction, as the means for communicating with the computer to prepare the lessons to be used by learners. Some author languages require extensive knowledge of computers and computer programming, while others require none.

CASE STUDY. A case study is a sample of real or fictitious events that ordinarily present a problem situation and some information that provides a vignette to illustrate a point. Typically, the students are asked to solve the problem developed in the case or to critique the solution presented.

CHAINING. A training strategy wherein the learning builds sequentially, enabling the student to tie together, or chain, the skills and knowledge acquired in one segment of the training to be built on in subsequent sections of the training.

COMPUTER AIDED INSTRUCTION (CAI). Also referred to as computer assisted instruction, computer based instruction, computer aided learning, and numerous other titles. All such names refer to the use of computers to present some or all of the training material to the learner. The computer mediates the instruction and usually maintains some kind of record of learner performance.

COMPUTER COURSEWARE. Training materials presented by computers in computer assisted instruction (CAI) are referred to as the courseware. It is the material presented to the students.

COMPUTER HARDWARE. The actual machines and other equipment associated with computers are referred to as the hardware component, or simply, the hardware.

COMPUTER SOFTWARE. The component of computer systems composed of computer programs is referred to as the software. The software is transparent to the users, but is essential for the computer to function. The software instructs the computer to perform certain functions in specific ways.

COURSE OBJECTIVE. A statement describing the expected behavior of the trainee at the completion of training. Good objectives are expressed in observable and measurable terms.

COURSE OVERVIEW. A brief summary of the course objectives and the methods to be used in the training.

CRITERION TEST. A test given at the end of a segment of training to determine whether the objectives of the training have been met.

DESK REVIEW. The initial test of the training materials, where the author or someone else reviews the training materials critically to determine whether the materials address the objectives and whether the presentation is appropriate to the target population.

DEVELOPMENTAL TEST. A presentation of the training to a group other than the intended target group to verify the flow, usability, timing, and other elements of the presentation. Several developmental tests may be necessary before the program is determined to be ready for the target population. The extent of developmental testing is often dependent on the numbers of students to be trained and the life expectancy of the program. A one-time training session is usually not tested as exhaustively as one that is to be used with large numbers of people over an extended period of time.

DISCRIMINATION. A training strategy that teaches via determining differences. This is a basic strategy and is effective when teaching learners to recognize problem or emergency situations.

EDUCATION. As contrasted with training, and in simplified terms, preparation for life (see *Training*).

ENABLING OBJECTIVE. Enabling objectives might also be called prerequisite objectives, since they need to be met before the course objectives can be achieved. For example, one should understand the concept of time before learning to use a clock.

FEEDBACK. Giving the learner information regarding his or her performance—providing knowledge of the results of their actions.

FIELD TRYOUT. A training program is tested using the developed materials on a group representative of the target population under the same conditions that the final version of the program is to be used. Field tryout occurs when a new program has been developed and when substantial changes have been made to an existing one, prior to final revision and implementation.

JOB AIDS. Devices that are designed to help the worker perform on the job after training, that are not part of the tool kit required for job performance. For example, a metric conversion chart could be a useful job aid to a draftsman or an engineer.

JOB DESCRIPTION. A definition of the tasks, duties, and responsibilities of the person doing the job in question. A job description can be helpful in determining the initial scope of the training plan.

LESSON PLAN. The aids used by the instructor as a guide through the materials used in the classroom. Lesson plans may be in the form of a skeleton outline, a detailed outline, an annotated outline, a script to be read verbatim, or a combination. Lesson plans may also consist of handwritten notes prepared by instructors to guide them through the lesson.

PROGRAM MAINTENANCE. Keeping the materials up to date and complete after they have been completed and implemented.

SELF-ADMINISTERED TRAINING. Any program that a learner may complete without intervention from an instructor or administrator is considered to be self-administered. Correspondence courses, computer assisted instruction programs, and some forms of written materials are usually self-administered.

SELF-PACED TRAINING. Training that permits the learners to proceed at their own individual rates is called self-paced, as contrasted with lock-step where all the learners proceed through the materials together. Self-paced may be self-administered or delivered by instructors.

SIMULATION. A method used to present materials and activities that are difficult or impossible to achieve in actual circumstances. Simulation is a kind of "make believe" version of the real world, requiring similar, if not identical responses from the trainees in the simulated situation as in the real one. Simulation may require extensive equipment, as in astronaut training, or may require none as in some training for executive decision-making. Simulation permits assessment of alternative strategies that might otherwise be impossible or extremely hazardous.

SUBJECT MATTER EXPERT (SME). The SME is the person who provides the job knowledge and substantive content to the training developer. The training developer may perform a task analysis to acquire a certain knowledge of the job, but the SME is familiar also with the operational details of the work and can help the training developer immeasurably. Intelligent use of SMEs permits training developers to prepare useful training materials on subjects about which they previously knew nothing.

TARGET POPULATION. The people who will ultimately be trained using the materials prepared by the training developer are known as the target population. The target population has identifiable characteristics, such as age, education level, reading ability, and prior experience that help the training developer prepare materials specifically for that group.

TASK ANALYSIS. A rigorous examination of specific work activities that identifies the actions of the job incumbent and the conditions under which each activity is to occur. While there is no best way to perform and report task analyses, they are essential to the training development process.

TEACH AND TEST METHOD. This refers, simply, to the method of presenting a small segment of training and then following it with a test to determine whether the trainee met the objective of the segment. The difference between this and other methods of testing is the frequency of testing and the levels of detailed knowledge required. For example, teaching Morse Code might be done using this technique, where each letter or small groups of letters are presented and tested before moving on to the next set.

TRAINING. Preparation for a specific job or set of tasks and activities relating to work (see *Education*).

TRAINING AIDS. Devices used to assist the trainees to learn the materials are referred to as training aids. They are generally used only during the training and not on the job. When these kinds of aids are used on the job, they are referred to as job aids. Training aids and job aids may, in fact, be identical in form and content. When they are used determines their nomenclature.

TRAINING PREREQUISITES. This term refers to a description of the kinds and amounts of previous experience, training, skill, and knowledge required for a trainee to undertake the training under consideration. For example, the ability to speak English fluently could be stated as a training prerequisite to a course in public speaking in the United States.

VISUALS. Collectively, all charts, tables, graphs, and text that are used in presentation of the training. The materials may be projected on a screen or a wall or may be in printed form in a book or enlarged and hung on a wall or stand.

Index